YORK NOTES

Jane Eyre

Charlotte Brontë

Notes by Sarah Rowbotham

Long

 York Press

YORK PRESS
322 Old Brompton Road, London SW5 9JH

ADDISON WESLEY LONGMAN LIMITED
Edinburgh Gate, Harlow,
Essex CM20 2JE, United Kingdom
Associated companies, branches and representatives throughout the world

First published 1998
Second impression 1998

ISBN 0-582-36832-4

Designed by Vicki Pacey, Trojan Horse, London
Illustrations by Kenny McKendry
Phototypeset by Gem Graphics, Trenance, Mawgan Porth, Cornwall
Colour reproduction and film output by Spectrum Colour
Produced by Addison Wesley Longman China Limited, Hong Kong

CONTENTS

Preface   **4**

PART ONE

INTRODUCTION   How to Study a Novel   **5**
Charlotte Brontë's Background   **6**
Context & Setting   **7**
Chronology of the Brontë Sisters   **10**

PART TWO

SUMMARIES   General Summary   **12**
Detailed Summaries, Comment,
    Glossaries & Tests   **14**
    Chapters 1–4   **14**
    Chapters 5–10   **21**
    Chapters 11–27   **29**
    Chapters 28–35   **49**
    Chapters 36–8   **59**

PART THREE

COMMENTARY   Themes   **64**
Structure   **70**
Characters   **71**
Language & Style   **78**

PART FOUR

STUDY SKILLS   How to Use Quotations   **80**
Essay Writing   **81**
Sample Essay Plan & Questions   **84**

PART FIVE

CULTURAL CONNECTIONS
    Broader Perspectives   **87**
    Further Reading   **87**

Literary Terms   **89**
Test Answers   **90**

PREFACE

York Notes are designed to give you a broader perspective on works of literature studied at GCSE and equivalent levels. We have carried out extensive research into the needs of the modern literature student prior to publishing this new edition. Our research showed that no existing series fully met students' requirements. Rather than present a single authoritative approach, we have provided alternative viewpoints, empowering students to reach their own interpretations of the text. York Notes provide a close examination of the work and include biographical and historical background, summaries, glossaries, analyses of characters, themes, structure and language, cultural connections and literary terms.

If you look at the Contents page you will see the structure for the series. However, there's no need to read from the beginning to the end as you would with a novel, play, poem or short story. Use the Notes in the way that suits you. Our aim is to help you with your understanding of the work, not to dictate how you should learn.

York Notes are written by English teachers and examiners, with an expert knowledge of the subject. They show you how to succeed in coursework and examination assignments, guiding you through the text and offering practical advice. Questions and comments will extend, test and reinforce your knowledge. Attractive colour design and illustrations improve clarity and understanding, making these Notes easy to use and handy for quick reference.

York Notes are ideal for:
- Essay writing
- Exam preparation
- Class discussion

The author of these Notes, Sarah Rowbotham, is currently an English examiner for one of the largest examination bodies. She teaches English in a large comprehensive school in Sheffield. Her previous York Note title is *Nineteenth Century Short Stories*.

The text used in these Notes is the new Penguin Classics edition, published 1996, edited by Michael Mason.

Health Warning: **This study guide will enhance your understanding, but should not replace the reading of the original text and/or study in class.**

PART ONE

INTRODUCTION

HOW TO STUDY A NOVEL

You have bought this book because you wanted to study a novel on your own. This may supplement classwork.

- You will need to read the novel several times. Start by reading it quickly for pleasure, then read it slowly and carefully. Further readings will generate new ideas and help you to memorise the details of the story.
- Make careful notes on themes, plot and characters of the novel. The plot will change some of the characters. Who changes?
- The novel may not present events chronologically. Does the novel you are reading begin at the beginning of the story or does it contain flashbacks and a muddled time sequence? Can you think why?
- How is the story told? Is it narrated by one of the characters or by an all-seeing ('omniscient') narrator?
- Does the same person tell the story all the way through? Or do we see the events through the minds and feelings of a number of different people?
- Which characters does the narrator like? Which characters do you like or dislike? Do your sympathies change during the course of the book? Why? When?
- Any piece of writing (including your notes and essays) is the result of thousands of choices. No book had to be written in just one way: the author could have chosen other words, other phrases, other characters, other events. How could the author of your novel have written the story differently? If events were recounted by a minor character how would this change the novel?

Studying on your own requires self-discipline and a carefully thought-out work plan in order to be effective. Good luck.

CHARLOTTE BRONTË'S BACKGROUND

Schooldays

Charlotte Brontë was born in 1816, the third daughter of a parson. The parsonage at Haworth in Yorkshire, a bleak and isolated place, was home for most of her life. Her father, Patrick Brontë, originally from Northern Ireland, was educated at Cambridge University, and reading and the pursuit of learning were encouraged at home. When Charlotte was very young her mother died; her elder sisters, Maria and Elizabeth, were sent with Charlotte to boarding school. The school was founded upon staunch religious principles and was harsh and austere. Charlotte retained very unhappy memories of this experience, especially since both her elder sisters died prematurely there. The depiction of the regimentation of Lowood and the tyrannical nature of Mr Brocklehurst are drawn directly from this period of her life. The tender portrait of the suffering Helen Burns has long been assumed to be a reminiscence of her eldest sister Maria, who did indeed die from consumption, as tuberculosis was then called.

Her childhood provides an autobiographical element in Jane Eyre.

Home life

Back at Haworth she was left in charge of her younger siblings, Emily, Anne, and Branwell. Apart from another spell at a different boarding school when she was fifteen, she remained at the parsonage, and the four children were left very much to their own devices. A dearth of external distractions meant that they turned to one another for entertainment and discourse. They were all immensely fond of literature and had very active imaginations, and the isolated nature of their lifestyle forced them to become almost total recluses, living and breathing the printed word and their own passion for imaginative writing. Their father discussed politics with them, they read his books and newspapers, and thus unavoidably became precocious, introverted children. This lifestyle fed into adulthood: without the society of others there was an extraordinarily strong emotional bond between the four; they spent every moment in each other's company. They became passionately immersed in the creation of imaginary worlds – Gondal and Angria – they wrote stories, plays and poetry together about the two worlds, as well as a periodical magazine which presented their rather slanted views on current events and invariably focused upon the latest news of the Duke of Wellington and Napoleon Bonaparte, their heroes.

Writing

It was in a sense inevitable that Charlotte, Emily and Anne became novelists. They were each avid readers and writers. However, to publish as a woman in the nineteenth century was extremely difficult; hence the pseudonyms of Currer, Ellis and Acton Bell which they adopted. Under these names Charlotte published *Shirley, Villette, The Professor* and *Jane Eyre*; Emily *Wuthering Heights*, and Anne *The Tenant of Wildfell Hall*. Some were received better than others; however all have now come to be regarded as major classics.

Teaching

As well as her writing, Charlotte also taught for much of her life: for three years at Roe Head school, and later as a governess in private households. She also studied and taught languages in Brussels. In 1854 she accepted her third offer of marriage and wed her father's curate. She died the following year.

CONTEXT & SETTING

The weather

The setting of *Jane Eyre* is vital to the plot and action, and often gives the reader an added dimension which helps our understanding of character and scene.

Consider the ways in which Charlotte Brontë involves the weather in the novel: there are numerous examples of climatic conditions intensifying mood (see **pathetic fallacy** in Literary Terms). The bleak view from the window in the opening section reinforces the idea of little Jane's unhappiness; 'a scene of wet lawn and storm-beat shrub, with ceaseless rain sweeping away wildly before a long and lamentable blast' (p. 14). The freezing conditions at Lowood add to the misery there in the same way that the storm in the Thornfield orchard on the night of Rochester's proposal gives a feeling of foreboding.

Charlotte Brontë based Thornfield Hall on a real place she had visited as a governess.

Charlotte Brontë was very much influenced by writers of **Gothic** (see Literary Terms) fiction, with its melodrama, haunted and gloomy castles, and innocent heroines. Thornfield is vaguely threatening with its sombre rooms hung with tapestry, its strange noises and mysterious secrets, and fits into this **genre** (see Literary Terms) very well: 'I lingered in the long passage … narrow, low, and dim, with only one little window at the far end … like a corridor in some Bluebeard's castle' (p. 122).

Social status

Social status was very important in the nineteenth century. Class divisions were far more fixed and pronounced than they are today. Jane is very conscious that, socially, she is inferior to many of those with whom she associates in spite of being a 'lady'. The idea that high social status does not necessarily mean goodness is an important **theme** (see Literary Terms and Commentary).

Surroundings

Houses and possessions are used to add information about characters. The Rivers are not wealthy and yet Jane approves of their home because it typifies the values of cleanliness and common sense: 'The parlour was rather a small room, very plainly furnished; yet comfortable, because clean and neat. The old-fashioned chairs were very bright, and the walnut-wood table was like a looking-glass … everything – including the carpet and curtains – looked at once well worn and well saved'

(p. 385). She is much more at home in this kind of environment than at the grand houses of Gateshead or Thornfield, and it is logical that she and Rochester should eventually settle at Ferndean Manor which is much less imposing than Thornfield Hall.

Women's status

Jane Eyre was written in 1847; therefore it is only just a few years into the Victorian period. Women had a very inferior status to men at this time, and few occupations were open to those who had to support themselves. Marriage was seen to be the only desirable goal, and was taken very seriously as a financial and business deal. Fathers gave their daughters large dowries when they married. Girls such as Jane had very few options open to them apart from using their education as a marketable resource. She is pragmatic enough to do this without complaint because she recognises that she has to be independent. Marriage is far from her thoughts up until the moment of Rochester's proposal. Her romantic, passionate nature would never settle for a marriage of convenience (see Themes).

Religion

Religious ideas and images are referred to frequently and are an integral element of the novel (see Themes). The religious context is significant because it was far more a part of everyone's day-to-day life than it is now. Nearly everyone went to church, said prayers at bedtime and studied the Bible. Jane is extremely religious and comes across several characters who are also governed by their religious beliefs.

1812	Patrick Brontë, an Irish Protestant clergyman marries Maria Branwell, a Cornish Methodist from Penzance
1813-8	Patrick publishes a collection of poems and two novels
1813 Birth of Maria	
Birth of Elizabeth **1815**	
Birth of Charlotte **1816**	
Birth of Branwell **1817**	
Birth of Emily **1818**	
1819	The Brontë family moves to Haworth in Yorkshire
Birth of Anne **1820**	
1821	Mrs Maria Brontë dies of cancer, and her sister Elizabeth Branwell comes to care for the children
Both Maria and Elizabeth die of tuberculosis at Cowan Bridge school **1825**	
1831	Charlotte boards at Roe Head school, Mirfield
1835-8	Charlotte returns to Roe Head as a teacher, with Emily as a pupil, but after three months of homesickness Emily returns to Haworth
1839	Charlotte, now a governess, visits Norton Conyers, near Rippon, model for Thornfield Hall. Charlotte turns down two proposals of marriage, both from clergymen
1841	Charlotte becomes governess to a family near Bradford

1842 — Charlotte and Emily study French in Brussels at Mme Heger's school

1843 — Charlotte returns to Brussels to teach and falls in love with Monsieur Heger

1844 — Charlotte returns home when her father becomes almost totally blind

1846 — *Poems by Currer, Ellis and Acton Bell* are published by the three sisters

1847 — Charlotte's *Jane Eyre* is published under the pseudonym of Currer Bell. Anne's *Agnes Grey* is published under the pseudonym of Acton Bell. Emily's *Wuthering Heights* is published under the pseudonym of Ellis Bell

1848 — Branwell dies of alcoholism. Emily dies of tuberculosis

Anne's *The Tenant of Wildfell Hall* is published

1849 — Anne dies of tuberculosis, leaving Charlotte as the only surviving sibling

Charlotte publishes *Shirley*

1850 — Charlotte meets writers of her day: Harriet Martineau, Mrs Gaskell, William Thackeray

1853 — Charlotte publishes *Villette*, based on her experiences in Brussels

1854 — Charlotte marries her father's curate, Arthur Nicholls

1855 — Charlotte is pregnant, but dies from a combination of ill health and pneumonia, before reaching full term

PART TWO

SUMMARIES

GENERAL SUMMARY

*Chapters
1–4*

*Gateshead – the
orphaned early
years.*

Jane Eyre is an orphan. Both her parents have died within a year of her birth, leaving her to the care of a maternal aunt, Mrs Reed of Gateshead. Mrs Reed is a widow, whose husband was the brother of Jane's mother. Before his death he made his wife promise to care for the child and bring her up as lovingly as their own three children. Mrs Reed keeps her promise only narrowly: she feeds, clothes and houses the little girl. She resents her mightily, however, and treats her cruelly and harshly. As the novel opens, Jane is ten years old, withdrawn and unloved, but high-spirited and with a strong sense of justice. Her resentment of the harsh treatment meted out by her aunt and cousins manifests itself in severe temper outbursts, which shock and outrage Mrs Reed so much that she arranges for Jane to be sent away to a charity boarding school.

*Chapters
5–10*

Lowood – school.

Jane spends eight years at Lowood. The first period is demanding and harsh. Living conditions are terrible: there is never enough food or heating, and many children sicken and die from a severe bout of typhus fever, exacerbated by their weakened state. Mr Brocklehurst, the head of the institution, is a cruel man whose misguided religious ideas about how to build character and feed the soul soon find fault amongst the general population and the school is taken over by more benevolent minds. This second period is more nurturing; Jane flowers under good conditions and sound teaching, and at the end of her stay there is one of the teachers herself, respected and loved, with a strong sense of personal integrity.

Chapters
11–27
Thornfield – life
and love begin.

At the age of eighteen she seeks independence in the form of a position of governess in a private household; a search which brings her to Thornfield, the home of Mr Rochester and his ward. From a prolonged absence Mr Rochester, some twenty-five years her senior, returns home to meet and fall in love with Jane. Despite their social inequality he insists upon marriage to her. Just at the point when the fairytale is about to become reality – actually at the altar – the marriage is abruptly halted by an announcement that Mr Rochester has a wife living, and therefore is attempting to commit bigamy. This discovery of 'the madwoman in the attic' nearly destroys Jane along with her hopes of happiness; in spite of Mr Rochester's pleas and protestations and her devoted love for him, she cannot accept the situation and flees Thornfield rather than consent to be his mistress.

Chapters
28–35
Marsh End –
adulthood and the
road to knowledge.

Penniless and almost starving, Jane roams the countryside in search of work and sustenance. She stumbles upon a house one night when the last of her strength is about to forsake her; the occupants admit her and save her from death. St John, Diana and Mary Rivers restore her to health and fitness and they become her family. It turns out that they are in fact cousins and when an unexpected inheritance falls to Jane she insists on sharing it equally with them, allowing her to repay their kindness and enabling all four to become financially independent at last.

During Jane's long months of absence from Thornfield, Mr Rochester has never left her thoughts for long. She knows that whilst he has a wife living she can never be with him, and mourns the loss of their love deeply. St John offers her a proposal of marriage and an invitation to travel with him to India to be a missionary, which she considers for a while, but the desire to be near Mr Rochester keeps her in England. One night, when she is being pressed by St John into making a decision, she 'hears' a voice crying for her in despair.

Chapters 36–8
The journey home.

Without hesitation she returns to Thornfield, finding it a blackened ruin and the mad Mrs Rochester dead. Her search for her love eventually leads her back to Mr Rochester, now blinded and partially crippled. The novel ends with their marriage and the prospect of a peaceful, contented life ahead.

DETAILED SUMMARIES

CHAPTERS 1–4: GATESHEAD – THE ORPHANED EARLY YEARS

CHAPTER 1

At the opening of the novel Jane Eyre is ten years old. She lives in a very grand house with her aunt, Mrs Reed, and this lady's three children: Master John, Eliza and Georgiana. We quickly discover that Jane is a most unhappy little girl. From the start her sense of loneliness and isolation is evident in the way she hides herself behind thick curtains in a deserted room,

Note how the pictures in the book add to the creation of mood.

ostracised by her aunt and cousins. She muses on her relief that the weather is too inclement for any possibility of a walk, and spends her time studying a book, Bewick's *History of British Birds*, whose pictures fascinate her. When she is discovered there by cousin John, he is cruel and abusive to her. Her resulting anger and refusal to be dominated are severely punished – she is carried away by servants to 'the red room' and locked in there.

COMMENT

It is quickly apparent that Jane has a strong personality and is beginning to question the behaviour and attitudes of those around her. Although young, she refuses to be dominated by her elder, male cousin; she recognises him for the bully that he is and stands up to his cruelty.

Her independence and strength of character is shown in well-defined opinions. Lashing out verbally and physically at cousin John is indicative of her strong nature and desire to be treated fairly.

The weather outside is cold, wet and miserable: 'near, a scene of wet lawn and storm-beat shrub, with ceaseless rain sweeping away wildly before a long and lamentable blast' (p. 14). There is **pathetic fallacy** (see Literary Terms) in the reflection of Jane's situation in the miserable weather. Also the gloomy pictures in the book fascinate her as they also mirror her situation.

GLOSSARY   **moreen** ribbed woollen
            Pamela famous eighteenth-century novel by Samuel
            Richardson, and popular reading for young women in the
            Brontës' time

CHAPTER 2   Bessie and Abbot, two of the servants, carry Jane to the red room, an old disused bedroom. It was here that Mrs Reed's husband, Jane's uncle, died some nine years before. Jane is clearly terrified about the prospect of being locked in this room with all its gloomy associations, but initially bears her punishment with fortitude. She is still extremely distressed and angry, and ponders on the unjust treatment she habitually receives from her family. She accepts that she is unwanted and unloved and does not fit in at Gateshead at all.

Note the author's use of descriptive language in relation to setting.

As she calms down, she becomes more aware and more afraid of her surroundings. Light fails and she becomes convinced that the room is haunted and screams out for help. Although the servants come to her aid, they are unsympathetic, and Mrs Reed insists that Jane be thrust bodily back inside the room and the door locked behind her. At this point Jane passes out from terror.

COMMENT

Jane's personality becomes clearer in this chapter; at ten years old she is able to look at her situation and judge it very honestly. She recognises that it is not her fault that she is being punished, and that her aunt and cousins resent her terribly for being an unwanted burden. She sees their cruelty and is very angry – '"Unjust! – unjust!" said my reason' (p. 22).

This is obviously a terrible punishment to inflict upon a little girl. She is clearly desperate and very afraid, but Mrs Reed has absolutely no sympathy for her. Seen through Jane's eyes she is clearly a cruel woman; however, even Jane admits that Mrs Reed sincerely believes that Jane is artful and wicked, therefore it is a just punishment in this lady's eyes.

GLOSSARY

Abigail old-fashioned word for maid

Poor-house charitable institutions which fed and housed destitute people

CHAPTER 3

Jane wakes up in her own bed in the nursery, confused and afraid. Her 'fit' has left her weak and disorientated. Gradually she becomes aware that there are two people with her – Bessie and Mr Lloyd, an apothecary. Bessie is gentle and kind towards her, giving her many

*Consider how we
can tell the
apothecary is
sympathetic to
Jane's situation.*

unwonted treats. However, the miserable truth of her situation affects her so that all the kindness in the world will not cheer her spirits.

Mr Lloyd also treats her kindly. When he revisits her the next day he questions her closely about her obvious depression. Although she is too young to analyse and articulate her feelings properly, she tells Mr Lloyd enough for him to recognise that she is unhappy at Gateshead and that to be sent away to school would benefit her greatly.

COMMENT

The adult **narrator** Jane (see Literary Terms) recognises the shrewdness in Mr Lloyd that the child does not understand. He clearly agrees that her treatment at Gateshead is harsh and unfair, and is trying to help her by suggesting the idea of school.

The **theme** (see Literary Terms) of being judged and consequently rewarded or punished in life because of physical appearances begins to be addressed in this chapter. Note how aware Jane is of her weak and unappealing features, and how unfavourably compared to Miss Georgiana (p. 34). However, rather than accepting this, there is an implicit sense of her reacting very strongly to the unfairness of such a surface judgement.

GLOSSARY

apothecary medical practitioner licensed to give medicines but inferior to doctor

Gulliver's Travels novel by Jonathan Swift about a journey involving three races of strange imaginary peoples, one of which was miniature in size

Guy Fawkes leader of a plot to overthrow the government by blowing up the Houses of Parliament

CHAPTER 4

Although Jane knows that Mr Lloyd has suggested school to Mrs Reed, she waits in vain for any further news on the subject. Christmas comes and goes – a

GATESHEAD – THE ORPHANED EARLY YEARS

terrible time for any child who is unloved and unwanted. She is excluded from all the celebrations and has to take all her meals alone. Her sense of her own strength becomes more and more evident, however. She refuses to be bullied by John any more, and hits him hard when he once again attempts to be cruel to her. When her aunt admonishes her for this, she is undaunted and argues back vehemently.

Jane's description of Brocklehurst shows her a good judge of character.

Eventually, the shadowy spectre of Mr Brocklehurst appears. He is the warden of Lowood charity school. Mrs Reed has been making enquiries and arrangements for Jane to be sent away. This man's interrogation of Jane reveals him to be someone harsh and cruel who is guided by staunch religious fervour. To Jane's childish eyes he reminds her of the wolf in the fairy story 'Little Red Riding Hood': 'what a great nose! and what a mouth! and what large prominent teeth!' (p. 41).

When he leaves, Jane and Mrs Reed have their final terrible encounter. Jane's emotional but honest account of her treatment shocks and undermines her aunt's authority. The power balance has finally shifted because Jane presents the truth fairly and honestly.

COMMENT

The childish reference to Little Red Riding Hood shows that Jane has instinctively made Brocklehurst both a figure of threat and one of mockery. He is diminished in our eyes by this reaction from her.

Jane's need for and belief in love is highlighted by her behaviour towards the little doll she cherishes, despite its shortcomings. It is a reflection of herself: small, shoddy in appearance, almost pitiful, but still worth attention and care.

As this phase of the novel draws to its conclusion there is a strong sense of Jane's developing integrity. Her opinions are firmer and more readily expressed, and people listen to them. Bessie's need for reassurance from Jane highlights this shift in relationship clearly.

Mrs Reed is shocked to the core by Jane's words not simply because of their vehemence but by their unarguable truth. Jane's character upholds the value of truth and honesty in all things, and this idea is to become a driving **theme** (see Literary Terms) in the novel.

GLOSSARY   **homily** sermon

curl-paper slips of paper serving a similar function to hair curlers

Identify the speaker.

1 'she really must exclude me from privileges intended only for contented, happy, little children'

4 'Do you know where the wicked go after death?'

2 'Have you any relations besides Mrs Reed?'

3 'What would uncle Reed say to you, if he were alive?'

Identify the person 'to whom' this comment refers.

5 'one really cannot care for such a little toad as that'

6 'his features were large, and they and all the lines of his frame were equally harsh and prim'

7 'this little girl has not quite the character and disposition I could wish'

Check your answers on page 90.

 Consider these issues.

a Why Mrs Reed is so cruel to Jane.

b Why the servants Bessie and Abbot strongly prefer the misses Reed so much.

c Why Master John is described so unfavourably.

d What we discover about the Reeds from their behaviour towards Jane.

e If there are any clues that Jane is not the wicked girl they think she is.

f What Mr Lloyd thinks of her and her situation.

CHAPTERS 5–10: LOWOOD – SCHOOL

CHAPTER 5

Sympathy for Jane is created by drawing attention to her isolation.

The second phase of the novel opens with the first of Jane's solitary journeys: journeys which signpost every change in her life. She travels to Lowood school alone and friendless. When she arrives she has her first meeting with the lovely Miss Temple whom she instantly recognises as someone to admire and trust.

Her first day at Lowood is spent in observation – one of Jane's most familiar occupations. What she observes troubles her in part: she sees the harsh treatment of the girls, the bad food, the regimented systems. However, she does not appear afraid or daunted by any of this.

Her first meeting with the remarkable Helen Burns takes place; again, Jane clearly recognises another kindred spirit. She is, however, confused by Helen's acceptance of a seemingly unjust punishment.

COMMENT

With all literature, a character's response to those around them is often a good indicator of their own personality. Jane is instantly drawn to Miss Temple and Helen Burns, and in their own ways both have profound effects on her life. Miss Temple is to become a role model for Jane, upholding the values of strength, observance of duty and above all truth to oneself which Jane recognises in herself.

Helen, interestingly, troubles Jane although she admires her intensely. She immediately recognises someone with strong opinions and personal integrity, and is confused by the seeming acquiescence to orders and duty even when misplaced.

GLOSSARY

brown stuff frocks cheap, hard-wearing, unflattering dresses
Babel clamour of tongues reference to the biblical story of the Tower of Babel

LOWOOD – SCHOOL

Rasselass novel by Samuel Johnson, actually spelled *Rasselas*, and very difficult for a young person to read

CHAPTER 6

The weather plays an important part in adding to the harsh conditions.

This chapter reinforces the cruelty of the regime at Lowood, again strengthened by the depiction of harsh weather conditions. The girls are given very little to eat, suffer extremely cold temperatures, work long hours, and have little discourse with each other.

Jane makes more headway with her relationship with Helen Burns, questioning her closely about her beliefs. It becomes apparent that Helen will bear with fortitude any cruelty and punishment without complaint. Jane struggles with this idea, believing that one should stand up to oppression and undeserved cruelty. Helen presents her with an alternative point of view, driven by the Christian conviction that one should bear any amount of suffering in this world in order to benefit in the afterlife. She accepts all the criticism and anger of her teachers, believing that they are right to correct and punish her for what seem to Jane to be petty and irrelevant misdemeanours.

COMMENT

Jane's constant questioning of Helen marks her as someone very interested in life and her place in it. She is a strong character who will not merely accept things as they are but wishes to explore and understand them. Her analytical nature is very well developed in one so young, and demonstrates her independence of mind.

Although intrigued and fascinated by Helen, and obviously very much in awe of her, she still does not blindly accept Helen's way of perceiving the world. Her innate sense of self allows her to construct her own opinions rather than slavishly adhering to those of others.

GLOSSARY   **skein of thread** unwound loop of thread or wool

CHAPTER 7

Jane spends the next three months endeavouring to 'fit into' the Lowood regime, however critically she surveys its shortfalls. Far from being self-pitying, she stands up with determination to the cold, the long hours, and strives to work hard and achieve success. The good opinion of her teachers and peers is very important to her, and she begins to earn this with her quick mind and strenuous attempts to learn.

*Note the **ironic** timing of Brocklehurst's wife's and daughters' visit.*

Then the event she has most dreaded happens. Mr Brocklehurst, with his wife and daughters, pays a visit of inspection to the school. Jane fears that he will destroy the good opinion she has managed to earn by telling everyone 'the truth' about her from Mrs Reed. This indeed happens; he denounces her as a liar and makes her stand in full view of the whole school. Her worst nightmare has come true.

COMMENT

Jane assumes that Mr Brocklehurst, as the figurehead of the school, is respected and admired by all. Reading between the lines, however, his hypocrisy is clearly apparent. His wife and daughters are arrayed in the finest clothes and jewels although he believes that the way to a pure soul is to punish the body: note how he demands that a girl with naturally curly hair has it all cut off because it will lead to vanity!

When he admonishes Miss Temple for her profligacy in allowing the children a simple meal because their breakfast had been ruined, we see in her manner an underlying disrespect for his severity. This is another indication that Mr Brocklehurst does not in fact command the respect which Jane assumes he merits.

GLOSSARY   **Chilblains** sore, inflamed, swollen areas on feet or hands, caused by extreme temperatures
hebdomadal weekly
chemises petticoats
tuckers white linen collars
top-knots hair buns

CHAPTER 8   Lost in isolation and despair, Jane is sought by Helen Burns who offers her comfort by telling her that Mr Brocklehurst is not admired, respected or even liked by the school – therefore no-one actually believes the accusations levelled against Jane. Miss Temple seeks the girls and invites them to tea in her room. She questions Jane closely about her time at Gateshead, and believes her account of the cruelty she suffered there. However, she promises to write to Mr Lloyd to have Jane's story corroborated.

Note Jane's appreciation of warmth and intelligence between women.

The tea in the teacher's room is a joy for Jane. She listens enraptured to Miss Temple and Helen's intellectual discussion, observing a real warmth and affinity between them. The reply from the apothecary indeed validates Jane's story, and she is publicly exonerated from all charges against her, to her sheer relief and the pleasure of her teachers and peers.

COMMENT   Helen and Jane have conflicting views on the importance of the opinions of others. Whilst Jane prizes public approval above all things, Helen feels that personal integrity is more important. This conflict is eventually resolved in the adult Jane, who listens to herself first but still needs the love and respect of those she admires.

A shadow is cast over the evening by a growing awareness that Helen is ill, and that Miss Temple is clearly extremely concerned about her. Reading as observers we are once again able to interpret in a way that Jane cannot. There is a sense of foreboding in Miss Temple's manner towards Helen: 'it was Helen her eye followed to the door; it was for her she a second time breathed a sad sigh; for her she wiped a tear from her cheek' (p. 86).

GLOSSARY

Slattern someone dirty, untidy
phylactery written reminder or sign

CHAPTER 9

Jane isolates herself from the danger. Look for other places where she does this.

As Jane becomes more settled at Lowood, the better weather reflects her altered state of mind. The year drifts into a warm spring and the mood looks set to alter. However, the warmth and damp bring a severe outburst of typhus fever to Lowood; the whole school becomes a hospital as more and more girls sicken and die from the extremely infectious fever.

Jane happily escapes from the illness; Helen, however, has developed consumption and is near to death. This she faces with the same undaunted spirit; her strength gives Jane courage and when she dies, Jane is at her side.

COMMENT

This extremely moving part of the story is described in a pragmatic, unemotional manner. No comment is made regarding Jane's feelings; a short passage describes the place where Helen is laid to rest and the simple inscription on her headstone, one assumes by Jane herself, fifteen years later. By not wallowing in the emotional intensity, the loss of Helen is made all the more poignant: as if no words are necessary or appropriate to honour her memory and the manner of her death. The reader is left with the **image** (see Literary Terms) of the two girls clinging to each other for support and warmth, which is tender and lovely on its own, needing no lengthy emotional outpourings to reinforce it.

GLOSSARY   **holm** low land near a stream

consumption tuberculosis or TB, disease of the lungs, once fatal but now curable

CHAPTER 10

The devastating effects of the typhus epidemic cause public notice to be brought to Lowood. Shocked by the harsh conditions there, the school is taken over by kinder minds. Jane skims over the next eight years, six as a pupil and two as a teacher, mentioning her success and happiness at the school, which ends with the marriage and departure of her role model Miss Temple. This event causes her to become restless, and she advertises for a situation as governess. Her first knowledge of Thornfield comes in a letter from Mrs Fairfax, the housekeeper there, offering her a position.

Jane's indepen-dence is beginning to be developed as she grows older.

Bessie the servant comes to visit her, telling her that her uncle came to the house some seven years before to look for her. He was on his way to the island of Madeira and could not stay long enough to seek her out. Jane also hears that the Reeds' situation is not a happy one: news which surprises neither her nor the reader.

COMMENT   This chapter serves to fill in the next eight years of Jane's life, as well as bridging the gap between Lowood and Thornfield. Her innate restlessness is very transparent here; Jane is on a quest for happiness and

The adult Jane is showing herself to be pragmatic and realistic about herself and her prospects.

fulfilment, no matter how much she denies this to herself.

Note Jane's desire for good opinion: in spite of impressing Bessie mightily with her accomplishments, she is still hurt by the notion that she is not physically appealing.

The hint of other relations who may be beneficial is not dwelt upon by Jane, although to the careful reader this is a significant piece of information.

GLOSSARY

testimonial character reference

Madeira an island off the coast of North Africa

Identify the speaker.

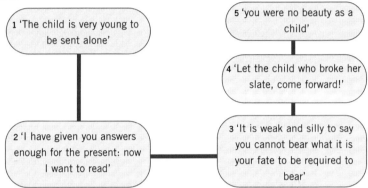

1 'The child is very young to be sent alone'

5 'you were no beauty as a child'

4 'Let the child who broke her slate, come forward!'

2 'I have given you answers enough for the present: now I want to read'

3 'It is weak and silly to say you cannot bear what it is your fate to be required to bear'

Identify the person 'to whom' this comment refers.

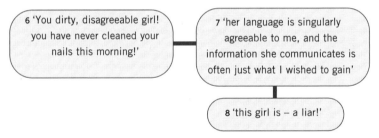

6 'You dirty, disagreeable girl! you have never cleaned your nails this morning!'

7 'her language is singularly agreeable to me, and the information she communicates is often just what I wished to gain'

8 'this girl is – a liar!'

Check your answers on page 90.

Consider these issues.

a Why Jane is immediately drawn to Helen Burns and Miss Temple.

b How the reader is directed to sympathise with the cruel treatment of the children.

c The hints that Mr Brocklehurst is a man to be scorned rather than respected.

d The places where Jane's growing independence of mind begins to show itself.

e Possible reasons for Miss Temple staying at Lowood when she disagrees with the rules of the school.

f Why Jane is so powerfully affected by Helen's death.

CHAPTERS 11–27: THORNFIELD – LIFE AND LOVE BEGIN

CHAPTER 11

Look at the way she reasons with herself whenever she is afraid or unsure.

The third phase of Jane's life opens with another solitary journey – this time to Millcote, the nearest town to Thornfield. Whilst waiting for her ride to the house she reflects upon her situation and muses that whilst on one level to be alone is terrifying, there is also a thrill of the unknown about it.

Her arrival at Thornfield is a pleasant one. She is greeted by the friendly Mrs Fairfax whom she still assumes to be the owner. She is astonished the following morning to learn that this lady is only the housekeeper and that Thornfield actually belongs to the elusive Mr Rochester.

She meets her pupil: the little French girl Adèle, Mr Rochester's ward. In her customary manner she asks many questions of Mrs Fairfax and so begins to get the measure of Thornfield Hall. The chapter ends with strange noises from a room on a distant floor of the house, and the first mention of the mysterious name Grace Poole.

COMMENT   The fact that this is a distinct new phase of Jane's story is signalled in the opening lines: 'A new chapter in a novel is something like a new scene in a play' (p. 108). The manner of narration is also different: note how the reader is drawn far more into Jane's thoughts. Her internal workings of mind now become the focus of the story as she reaches maturity and is able to reflect more articulately on her own situation, rather than leaving readers to draw their own conclusions.

As ever, Jane is strongly influenced by her surroundings: her first full day at Thornfield opens with a survey of the pleasant aspect from her window which cheers her immensely and hints at a better life to come.

Her physical appearance is referred to: she examines her wish that she were more physically appealing, recognising this desire for what it is and dealing with it pragmatically.

GLOSSARY   **negus** a hot drink of port, sugar, lemon and spice
              On to the leads the gallery in the roof, lead referring to lead roof covering

CHAPTER 12

Jane recognises The first three months of her new situation pass
Adèle's faults but peacefully enough. She is reasonably contented with her
does not judge her lot, although she is aware of her restless spirit and quest
for them. for happiness. Her companions please her, and there is
a clarity and honesty in her reaction to them, as in her dispassionate response to Adèle.

This chapter contains the first, dramatic, meeting with Mr Rochester. She encounters him when he falls from his horse and she is obliged to give him assistance. Still unaware of who he is, she is amazed on returning home to discover that the gentleman she assisted in the road is in fact her employer.

COMMENT   Jane's future relationship with Rochester is most clearly set out in their first meeting. Although penniless, demure and socially dependent, she is not afraid of this rather gruff-looking man, but approaches him confidently to offer her help. She gives him physical assistance and support, which is a benchmark for their unusual relationship throughout. In spite of her apparent inferiority she maintains a strength and power in relation to him, a refusal to be dominated.

His dog Pilot she describes as a 'Gytrash', or spirit dog. Remember her experience in the red room of Chapter 3, when one of her visions in the fit was something with 'a great black dog behind him' (p. 27). Maybe the child Jane had a premonition, a hint that this event was to begin the most remarkable aspect of her life?

CHAPTER 13

Note in what ways Rochester's interest in Jane begin to show.

That evening Mr Rochester sends for Adèle and Jane. Adèle has been in a flurry of excitement all day, desperate for the opportunity to show off to her guardian. When the interview finally takes place, Jane feels instantly comfortable with Mr Rochester's abrupt manner and gruff composure. He questions her closely, refusing to flatter her although clearly impressed with her painting skills especially.

She discovers from Mrs Fairfax that there were some Rochester family troubles, and that he has to bear some kind of unhappiness, which partly explains why he seldom returns to Thornfield.

COMMENT Jane is not intimidated by Rochester although he is clearly a rude and abrupt man. Her opinions of him are honest and forthright; she appears to take the measure of him instantly. The hint of his being dissatisfied and gloomy is reinforced by his manner towards Adèle, which is certainly lacking warmth.

The description of Jane's paintings gives a very interesting insight into her character. All three present a dreamy and passionate side to Jane which must intrigue Rochester when faced with the demure and acquiescent young governess before him.

GLOSSARY   **break through one of your rings** a fairy ring
                     eulogiums overblown praise of character

CHAPTER 14

Now that Mr Rochester has again become resident and master of Thornfield, the house is busy with visitors. Jane sees him infrequently, and can never predict his manner towards her when they do chance to meet on a corridor or pathway.

Note the way neither is lost for words with each other and seems to get on well.

One evening he again sends for her and Adèle; the child is given a large box of gifts from Rochester's travels, and while she examines them in delight Jane and Rochester have their longest, most interesting conversation to date. He is frank and honest with her, as she is with him, and a large part of their **dialogue** (see Literary Terms) investigates the conventions of relationship between master and 'paid subordinate'.

COMMENT

The powerful communication between Rochester and Jane highlights the equality of mind they share, regardless of their positions in society. Jane is eloquent and articulate with him, and certainly not afraid to be honest: 'do you think me handsome?' – 'No, sir' (p. 149). He is refreshed and fascinated by her attitude of mind and refusal to be dominated.

Underneath the occasionally flippant tone and wordplay, they are examining each other closely. He is intrigued by her and the effect she has on him; her clarity enables him to be honest about himself. He wants to open up to her and is interested in her opinion of him.

GLOSSARY **Quaker** austere and severe religious order
philanthropist someone who devotes their life to benevolent, charitable acts

CHAPTER 15

Think how this information affects our opinion of Rochester.

This chapter uncovers the mystery surrounding Adèle's place at Thornfield. She is the illegitimate daughter of a Frenchwoman, one-time mistress of Mr Rochester. This women, Céline Varens, treated Rochester badly and was only really interested in his money. When the child came along he undertook her care, but does not believe she is his daughter. His motivation for looking after her is to purge some sin by committing a charitable deed, nothing more.

In bed that night thinking about Rochester's attitude towards her, Jane is disturbed by strange noises, and a 'demoniac laugh' (p. 168) outside her door. Investigating this, she discovers that Rochester's bed curtains are on fire and that he is nearly unconscious from smoke inhalation. She stirs and wakes him, managing to quench the fire and save his life. His gratitude towards her has an unwarranted warmth about it, and this section of the novel ends with her presentiment of his growing affection towards her.

COMMENT   Jane does not judge Rochester for his past life, although its 'worldliness' must be a shock. Rather, she is fascinated by his attitude towards his past deeds and also the impetus which apparently drives him to bare his soul to her. This is where the reader is in a better position to judge the situation than Jane; it is clear to us that Rochester is growing to care for Jane but her natural innocence and reticence does not allow her to see this.

Her attitude to his story shows her natural integrity and independence of mind. Instead of being condemnatory, she accepts that he has made mistakes and is more interested in his desire to change and reform.

GLOSSARY   **that metal welkin** that metal-coloured sky

                   chicken in the pip diseased

                   the curtains were on fire four-poster beds would have curtains around them

CHAPTER 16

Jane is beginning to become more and more fascinated by Rochester.

Jane passes the morning after the fire in a whirl of agitation. In spite of her pragmatic and sensible nature she is convinced that what she saw and heard in Rochester's tone and eyes was love. The day passes unremarkably. Jane has the opportunity to question Grace Poole regarding the events of the night before and is staggered by the woman's apparent composure and hypocrisy, believing as she does that Grace is the source of the strange noises and the cause of the fire. She entertains momentary suspicions regarding Grace's relationship to Rochester which she almost immediately dismisses as ridiculous.

Think what this action reveals about Jane's character.

When she learns that Rochester has left to visit friends, she is perturbed. Mrs Fairfax tells her of the beautiful Blanche Ingram who will be one of the party. It becomes instantly clear to Jane that her own suspicions regarding Rochester's feelings towards her are nothing more than childish fancy, and she seeks to destroy them by painting two portraits; one an imaginary one of Blanche which she makes as exquisite as possible, and one of herself which is plain and dowdy.

COMMENT   Jane's strength of character is keenly visible here. Although her growing love for Rochester is palpable to the reader, Jane refuses to fuel these feelings, and instead forces herself to stare reality in the face by painting the miniatures.

Rochester's sudden departure is difficult to interpret as we are not privy to his inner workings of mind; thus we have to think beyond Jane's interpretation of events and judge for ourselves why he may have left Thornfield – and her – so suddenly.

GLOSSARY   **Arraigned at my own bar** legal metaphor (see Literary Terms) meaning she is judging herself

plate in the plate-closet silver plate

CHAPTER 17

After two weeks of silence, a letter announces the imminent return of Rochester with a large party of guests. The whole house is made ready, and for three days there is a flurry of activity. Jane anxiously awaits the sight of Rochester and Blanche Ingram.

Think about what ideas we have at this point regarding the Thornfield mystery.

The mystery surrounding Grace Poole deepens as Jane overhears a whispered conversation between two maids regarding Grace's large salary and the difficult nature of her job. She discovers that she is being deliberately kept in the dark, but soon forgets to think of this as thoughts of Rochester take over.

The evening after the arrival of the party, Mr Rochester sends word for Adèle and Jane to come downstairs after dinner. Jane is extremely reluctant but Rochester is adamant. Whilst the guests entertain themselves, Jane is able to remain unobserved and studies Blanche and Rochester closely, interpreting the relationship between them as one of courtship. Seeing an opportunity to escape, she slips away but is intercepted in the hallway by Rochester and is unable to disguise her emotional distress.

COMMENT   Again the telltale signs of Rochester's feelings for Jane are clearly visible to the reader. The solicitous nature of his tone towards her, his demand that she be present with the party every evening, his sudden pause: 'Goodnight, my –' (p. 205) all clearly denote the behaviour of a man in love.

In contrast, note the ribaldry and flirtatious tone adopted in the conversation between him and Blanche Ingram: although entertaining and articulate, there is a lack of depth and sincerity already visible in their discourse with each other.

GLOSSARY   **pot of porter** beer

like a Dian Diana, the Greek goddess of hunting

CHAPTER 18

As the days progress, Jane has ample opportunity to observe and study the relationship between Blanche and Rochester. Her love for him deepens constantly, as does her horror at the dawning realisation that Blanche, in spite of being beautiful, accomplished and ladylike, is harsh and cold. When she realises that Rochester himself knows this and does not love her, she is devastated. She could have accepted the situation if there was genuine love between them, but is tormented at the idea that he will marry for 'family, perhaps political reasons; because her rank and connexions suited him' (p. 211).

Note Jane's unflattering description of Blanche's behaviour.

One gloomy evening, after Rochester has been away all day on business, first a Mr Mason arrives at Thornfield, then a beggar woman arrives desiring to tell the fortunes of all the young ladies. The guests gladly seize on this opportunity of distraction; Blanche, however, is clearly very disturbed by what she is told. The fortune-teller refuses to leave without an audience with Jane.

COMMENT

Here we fully appreciate the magnitude of Jane's feelings for Rochester; the selflessness of the love she feels for him. It never enters her head to include herself in any ideas of his future happiness, but she sincerely wants him to make a marriage of love for his own sake.

The cruel nature of Blanche Ingram is shown by her manner towards Adèle, and her haughty attitude to Jane.

Jane's control and calm in the face of a visit to the gypsy directly contrasts with the hysterical shrieks of some of the ladies, highlighting her dignity and personal integrity.

GLOSSARY

Paynim chivalric term for Muslim
beldame witch

CHAPTER 19

Jane has her interview with the 'gypsy' who attempts to draw her out and get her to give her opinions of the party, especially Rochester and Miss Ingram. The **dialogue** (see Literary Terms) between them grows stranger and stranger, until finally Jane realises that the gypsy is in fact Rochester in disguise.

She appears a little bemused by his behaviour but has no time to reflect upon it.

He reacts with stunned shock to the news that a Mr Mason from Jamaica has arrived at Thornfield; indeed, Jane has never seen him look so troubled, almost afraid.

However, the evening closes amicably enough, with Rochester apparently in jovial conversation with Mason as he escorts him to a guest room for the night.

COMMENT

The lovely initial banter between the 'gypsy' and Jane is far superior to similar **ironic** (see Literary Terms) conversations between Rochester and Blanche. Jane is clearly equal to Rochester in intellect, sense and feeling if not social status or age.

The fact that Jane has suspicions that the woman is Rochester in disguise is testament to how well she has studied him; she knows him much better than his 'fiancée'.

Whilst Jane has been keenly observing him, he has also been doing exactly the same with her; his comments display accurate and sensitive judgements of her personality and feelings. There is a sense of equality and balance in the way each has been privately observing the other.

GLOSSARY

rent-roll　bank balance

dished　'dished up' or got rid of

interlocutor　person with whom one has a conversation

CHAPTER 20

Look at the use of description to add to the sense of fear and panic.

The household is disturbed in the night by a terrible cry. Although Rochester manages to soothe everyone by claiming the noise is nothing more than a servant's nightmare, Jane is not convinced. She is right in her suspicions; Rochester calls her to his aid once again, this time to tend to Mr Mason, who has been viciously attacked, presumably by the strange Mrs Poole. Jane's courage is severely called upon as she has to stay by Mason for two hours in the dark whilst Rochester goes for a doctor. He has been forbidden to speak to her on any account.

Eventually Rochester returns with the doctor, and Mason is carried away. Jane and her employer walk in the gardens, and once again there is a warmth and tenderness in his manner towards her. However, he also asks whether she would be there to keep him company on the evening before his wedding to Miss Ingram; there is sarcasm and harshness in his tone when he mentions that name and subject.

COMMENT   The circumstances into which Jane is placed here would thrill and delight the nineteenth-century readers. The **Gothic** (see Literary Terms) setting with the invalid, the blood, the dark, the strange noises and mysterious threatening presence, all combine to create a sense of mystery and to highlight Jane's innocence and vulnerability.

Look for ways in which Jane indirectly criticises frivolous female behaviour.

Once again she is shown to be resourceful and courageous; the other ladies were practically hysterical at Mason's first shriek, but Jane copes with these terrible events with fortitude.

The strength of Rochester's feelings for her are even more palpable in this chapter, but Jane seems oblivious to them. When he speaks of the 'good and bright qualities ... all fresh, healthy, without soil and without taint' (p. 245), it is clearly Jane he refers to.

GLOSSARY   **volatile salts** smelling salts, used to revive lightheadedness
I shall wax dangerous turn dangerous, as the moon 'waxes and wanes'

CHAPTER 21

The next day Jane is sent for by her aunt Reed, who is near to death. Her son John has led a wild and irresponsible life, almost bringing his mother to financial ruin. News of his death has brought on a stroke, but she cannot rest until she has spoken to her niece.

Jane has a huge capacity for forgiveness.

After taking leave of Rochester and being entreated with a promise to return as soon as possible, Jane hastens back to Gateshead. Here she finds her cousins Eliza and Georgiana, both unlikeable and selfish women in their way, waiting impatiently for their mother's death so that they can resume their lives. Mrs Reed, as cold and austere towards Jane as ever, tells her that she received a request some three years before from Jane's uncle that she be sent to join him in Madeira. Mrs Reed hated Jane so much that she told this man that the child was dead. Although she still hates Jane, some pricking of the conscience has forced her to clear her mind of this action before she can die.

COMMENT

It comes as no surprise that the Reeds have not had successful lives: the implicit message being that selfishness and cruelty can only lead to misery. Jane is in the enviable position of being able to rise above them all and view them dispassionately because she recognises that she no longer needs or respects them.

Once again, her reaction to traumatic news is strange; she could have been living a very different life if only her aunt had acted more kindly but, as she would never have met Rochester in this case, any regret seems irrelevant. The chapter opens with her musing on the workings of fate, a strong idea in the novel.

Jane's growing strength of character and desire to do the right thing are reinforced here.

Note the nature of the conversation between her and Rochester at the beginning of this chapter: it is resonant with implied meaning, charged with emotion underneath the surface banter.

The recurrent dream of the baby is perhaps a **personification** (see Literary Terms) of the innocence and vulnerability of Jane herself; she has to be her own support and carer because she is alone in the world.

GLOSSARY   **sort of ruth** regret

amity friendship

the Rubric list or set of rules

CHAPTER *22*

Think about what evidence there is for Jane's self-control here.

Jane returns to Thornfield: another journey, this one a mixture of anticipation and fear for the future. The prospect of seeking a further job does not distress her; in fact she refuses to think that far ahead. She is too intent upon preparing herself for the pain she will feel when Rochester marries.

He is delighted to see her: his highly animated language and tone show this clearly. She is welcomed by Mrs Fairfax and Adèle, and two weeks pass tranquilly with no sign of any wedding preparations. Jane begins to hope and suspect that the marriage is not, in fact, going to take place.

COMMENT

Jane finally acknowledges her deep love for Rochester. She recognises that this much self-denial is futile and all her efforts to keep a check on her feelings will still not protect her from the pain of losing him.

The powerful force of her feelings for Rochester is intensified by the shift into **present tense** (see Literary Terms) as she approaches Thornfield (pp. 274–5). The effect of this technique is to remove the distance of time from Jane's narration, and make the event appear much more immediate.

GLOSSARY   **take the veil** become a nun

cynosure centre of attention

vicinage area, vicinity

ignis fatuus will-o'-the-wisp

THORNFIELD – LIFE AND LOVE BEGIN

CHAPTER 23

Setting is again very important to this moment. Think why the author chooses a lovely night for the proposal.

Taking a walk in the garden on a beautiful midsummer's evening, Jane becomes aware of Rochester's presence and tries to avoid him, feeling uncomfortable in his company. He has been watching her and is now apparently following her, and persuades her to walk with him in the orchard.

It is in this idyllic setting that the final truth of his feelings becomes clear; he denies the existence of any engagement to Miss Ingram and pleads instead for Jane's hand in marriage. At first aghast, she is transported into pure joy when she realises that he is being sincere and genuinely loves her.

COMMENT

Note again the **pathetic fallacy** (see Literary Terms) in the weather conditions, echoing and reinforcing Jane's happiness.

The sudden break in the weather resulting in the storm which splits the horse chestnut tree into two is a clear omen, signifying that this impending union is not right.

Look for other places where the reader is aware of more than Jane.

Rochester's manner and language also hint towards all not being well: the 'savagery' with which he holds to Jane and his defiance of 'the world's judgement' (p. 287) present a cause for concern. 'He set his teeth' (p. 284) in determination. However, Jane is oblivious to all this, so enraptured is she by this change in her fortunes.

It is reasonable to be slightly concerned by the way Rochester plays his game with Jane right up to the last minute: torturing her with the idea of his marriage to another. One interpretation of his behaviour is that he is forcing her into a confession of her real feelings in order to be sure that his suspicions are correct.

lady-clock ladybird

Mrs Dionysius O'Gall of Bitternutt Lodge clearly a sardonic name invented by Rochester

CHAPTER 24

The following morning Jane is anxious to see Rochester to make sure she has not dreamed the wonderful events of the previous evening. Mrs Fairfax is cool towards her, having witnessed an embrace between them, and Jane requests that she explain the truth to her immediately. Her caution is upsetting to Jane although Mrs Fairfax's worries are justified and reasonable, with a tinge of **ironic** (see Literary Terms) warning: 'I do fear there will be something found to be different to what either you or I expect' (p. 297).

Rochester takes Jane shopping, but she is uncomfortable with his attempts to shower her with expensive gifts. She feels that their relationship should not be transformed into a 'society match' by such trappings, and is equally uneasy with his repeated

Jane stands up to protestations of love towards her. She manages
Rochester in spite successfully to steer him away from sentimental
of being in love behaviour, and the month leading up to the marriage
with him. passes with her in control of the situation. She also decides to write to her uncle, feeling that some form of financial independence, however modest, would ease the discomfort she suffers due to the gap between them.

COMMENT   It is not easy to interpret the reasons for Jane's behaviour here. She loves Rochester desperately and completely: 'My future husband was becoming to me the whole world; and more than the world: almost my hope of heaven' (p. 307). Yet she shies away from his desire to lavish her with affection and gifts. She perhaps feels that he should love her for herself and not attempt to invalidate the relationship between them by making it appear the same as any other in his social circle. Also, her need to be true to herself and to be independent is a powerful aspect of her personality, not to be denied even when transported by love.

GLOSSARY   **Jew-usurer** the caricature of a calculating, manipulative money lender, familiar in literature

badinage French word meaning banter, a fun exchange of words

parterre formally patterned flower garden

seraglio harem

suttee Hindu custom where a widow burnt herself on her husband's funeral pyre

CHAPTER 25

The day before the wedding Jane is unsettled and restless. Again, the overcast and windy weather reflects her mood. She waits impatiently for Rochester to return home, eventually going to meet him and greeting him with unaccustomed warmth and sincerity.

Eventually she tells him that she had a very vivid dream which had a sense of omen about it. The dream again involved the idea of being burdened with a young child, and showed Jane and Rochester being separated for ever. She then tells him that on waking from this dream she discovered a strange, fearful woman in her room who tore her wedding veil apart before leaving the bedroom.

Look at Rochester's reaction to Jane's story and why she accepts his word in spite of her suspicions about his interpretation. Rochester is evidently much shaken by this, although he gives her a reasonable explanation for the occurrence, blaming Grace Poole once again and surmising that Jane was half asleep and did not recognise her. Although not convinced, Jane tries to appear mollified, and promises to sleep in the nursery with Adèle and Sophie, rather than remain in her own room and be afraid.

COMMENT   Rochester evidently has another motive for keeping Jane away from her own room; he senses a real threat to her safety and wants to keep her protected. There is more going on than Jane is aware of and the appearance of this strange woman frightens Rochester disproportionately, given his explanation of the mystery.

Again, physical events seem guided and influenced by spiritual, or even psychic features; the weather, Jane's dreams, signs and indicators are as much involved in the course of events as substantial concrete affairs.

CHAPTER 26

On the day of the wedding Rochester is hurried and restless, 'grimly resolute' (p. 322). Jane notices two strangers who enter the quiet church by a side door.

When the service comes to questioning whether there is 'any lawful impediment', one of the men steps forward. He is a lawyer who declares that Rochester has already a wife living at Thornfield Hall and is thus attempting to commit bigamy. It transpires that Jane's uncle knows Richard Mason, the brother of Mrs Rochester, and when Jane wrote to inform him of her impending marriage the alarm was raised.

Jane remains an observer as if she has retreated from her feelings in shock.

Rochester leads them all to the house where we are confronted by the spectre of the first Mrs Rochester – a mad woman, closeted in an attic under the guard of Grace Poole. She violently attacks him, apparently not for the first time.

Jane manages to preserve her calm in the face of all this information, only relinquishing her hold on her feelings when alone in her room. She has nothing now except her belief in God and herself.

THORNFIELD – LIFE AND LOVE BEGIN

COMMENT   Once the mystery is finally explained, much of the
          subtext (see Literary Terms) of the story so far becomes
          clear. Jane's sense of a mystery at Thornfield, the sight
          of the strange woman in her room, the fearsome attack
          on Richard Mason, the unearthly laughs and noises are
          all now in context.

          Rochester's behaviour is surely cause for scrutiny here.
          He calls upon a higher court than that of the world to
          judge whether he in fact was acting immorally, given
          his suffering since being tricked into marrying this
          woman for his family's financial gain. Jane does not
          judge him; she loves him too well and also believes in a
          similar kind of moral code.

GLOSSARY   **craft** witchcraft

CHAPTER 27

After a terrible period alone with her thoughts, Jane
stirs and looks about for an answer. The awful fact –
that she must leave Thornfield – is so horrendous that
she tries to turn from it, but it is the only possible
solution. During a passionate interview with Rochester
he pleads with her to run away with him, but she
refuses.

Do you think his
vague interpreta-
tion of the nature
of Bertha's
madness is
accurate? Think
about what might
influence it.

He tells her the full story of his marriage to Bertha
Mason. His father arranged it so that he would have a
fortune of his own, the Masons being a rich family who
would give a dowry of £30,000. It soon appeared that
she was insane, as was her mother, and Rochester lived
a terrible life with her in Jamaica before bringing her to
Thornfield and shutting her away. He then ran away to
Europe where he led a debauched and discontented life.

When he speaks of the effect Jane had upon him, we
see the full force, beauty and sincerity of his love for
her. She is almost powerless to resist this, but is

resolved to 'keep the law given by God, not by man'
(p. 356). Although it breaks her heart, she steals away
in the night.

COMMENT   This bravery in the midst of total despair is quite
astounding. Her sense of self is an intrinsic aspect of
her nature, and never is its force more keenly felt than
at the brink of temptation: '*I* care for myself. The more
solitary, the more friendless, the more unsustained I
am, the more I will respect myself' (p. 356). Her
fundamental creed is clearly established: 'Do as I do:
trust in God and yourself' (p. 355).

To a modern reader this adherence to a moral and
religious code at the expense of total happiness is hard
to appreciate; even some nineteenth-century readers
would struggle with her dilemma. Religious beliefs and
societal codes were far more influential than they
appear today, and Jane was acting under the fear of
disgrace and God's punishment.

*A rather
melodramatic
section where the
reader has to try to
see how Jane is
motivated, rather
than how we
might have
reacted.*

She forgives Rochester completely because she
understands the circumstances and because she sees
how much he loves her. He is acting under the
direction of an alternative moral code, not out of
immorality. In spite of this understanding she cannot
agree to his plan.

GLOSSARY   **temporary lapses** drunkenness. Grace Poole is clearly fond of
drink
will-o'-the-wisp phantom
Pigmy intellect very small, from the tribe of people noted for
being short

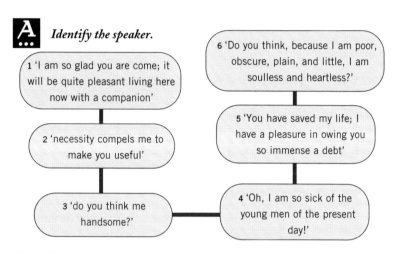

A *Identify the speaker.*

1 'I am so glad you are come; it will be quite pleasant living here now with a companion'

2 'necessity compels me to make you useful'

3 'do you think me handsome?'

4 'Oh, I am so sick of the young men of the present day!'

5 'You have saved my life; I have a pleasure in owing you so immense a debt'

6 'Do you think, because I am poor, obscure, plain, and little, I am soulless and heartless?'

Identify the person 'to whom' this comment refers.

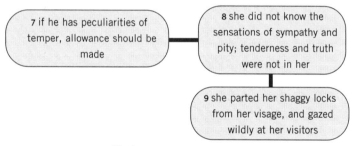

7 if he has peculiarities of temper, allowance should be made

8 she did not know the sensations of sympathy and pity; tenderness and truth were not in her

9 she parted her shaggy locks from her visage, and gazed wildly at her visitors

Check your answers on page 90.

B *Consider these issues.*

a The recurring **image** (see Literary Terms) of light and darkness, good and evil.

b Rochester continually describes Jane as something unworldly, of the 'air'.

c The difficulties presented to Jane in the month before the wedding which hint that all is not well.

d Recurrent reference to physical appearance; Jane has not yet become mature enough to be careless of this.

e The way Rochester treats Adèle coldly and what this shows of his character.

f His justification for behaving so cruelly towards Jane with Blanche.

CHAPTERS 28–35: MARSH END – ADULTHOOD AND THE
ROAD TO KNOWLEDGE

CHAPTER 28

All Jane's physical   Totally destitute and alone, Jane roams the countryside
and emotional   in search of some means of continued existence. She
strength is put to   looks about for work but finds nothing and no-one to
the test.   help her. Within a matter of hours she is reduced to
begging for scraps of food. Her innate pride and
delicacy is severely tested, but she still has enough sense
to recognise that the needs of the body must be
addressed. Several times she wishes for death, but the
thought of leaving the earth with Rochester still living
is anathema to her.

After three days spent in this terrible way, she sees a
candle shining feebly in the distance across a barren
heath. The house she approaches is her last hope; she
observes the inmates through the window and is driven
by some sense of their familiarity to knock and beg for
help. The servant Hannah drives her away, but the
master of the house finds her on the step and hearing
her call to God for help, is intrigued and brings her
inside.

MARSH END – ADULTHOOD AND THE ROAD TO KNOWLEDGE

COMMENT   The inherent **pathos** (see Literary Terms) of this chapter is very powerful. Jane does not wish to dwell on sordid details, but she relates enough for the reader to feel her suffering keenly. For one so independent to be forced into this position highlights the force of her integrity: she would rather suffer all this than be with the man she loves.

From a few minutes' observation she feels an empathy with the women within: 'I seemed intimate with every lineament' (p. 372). For some reason she senses a connection here: of course she is correct, and this reinforces our faith in her judgement and intuition.

GLOSSARY   **soliloquy** a character's spoken thoughts, meant only for speaker and audience

lexicon dictionary

CHAPTER 29

Jane passes three days at Moor House in a state of nervous collapse, tenderly nursed by Diana and Mary Rivers. She gradually regains her strength and is soon able to sit downstairs. The initial distrust of the servant Hannah is dissipated once they have a conversation and Hannah realises that Jane is honest, decent, and well educated, certainly not the fraudster she suspected.

Note the attention to detail in the descriptions of the Rivers and their home.

Diana and Mary continue to be fascinated by Jane but their sensitivity prevents them from asking too many questions. Their brother, however, is more forthright, and Jane feels it only fair that he be given as much honest explanation as possible without alluding to Rochester and Thornfield. He appears satisfied with what she tells him and promises to do what he is able to find her honest work.

COMMENT   Mary and Diana seem to recognise the same fellow-feeling in Jane as she does in them; they warm to her instantly and trust her absolutely. Their kindness and generosity is plain.

St John evidently respects Jane for her honesty and integrity. He is studying her and is satisfied with what he sees.

Notice Jane's approval of the house: plain and functional, yet clean and warm. This is another example of her sensible value judgements which care nothing for fancy trappings and rich adornments.

GLOSSARY   **nursed** wet-nursed, a common practice amongst gentry in the last century

solus alone

Quiescent quiet

insensible unaware

torpor totally relaxed, unconscious

CHAPTER 30

Jane continues to delight in the company of Diana and Mary. The three have remarkably similar tastes and attitudes, and a strong bond of affection quickly develops.

Notice how the author builds up her gloomy picture of St John.

Three weeks pass, during which Jane hears nothing from St John about the promised employment. In her customary manner she continues to observe him closely, and discovers him to be fiercely religious. His church sermons distress her because they are so fervent and smack of someone desperately searching for a way to devote his life wholeheartedly to God.

Eventually he tells her that he needs someone to set up a small school for girls in the nearby village of Moreton. She leaps at this opportunity, much to his pleasure.

MARSH END – ADULTHOOD AND THE ROAD TO KNOWLEDGE

A letter comes with news of the death of the Rivers' uncle; some family disagreement means that he has not left his fortune to them but to another, unnamed relative. The sisters have to leave home to return to their jobs as governesses, and Jane prepares to start her school.

COMMENT   The observant reader will have of course picked up the link between Jane's ailing uncle John and the Rivers' recently deceased uncle John. However, this information, like so much else of the mystery, is left in the air until such time as all the threads of the story can be bound together.

The Rivers respond to life in much the same way that Jane does.

The Rivers respond pragmatically to the news that they have been left without what should surely have been their legacy. Their lives would have been made much happier with even a little money, instead of which the sisters have to return to their hated professions in unfriendly households.

Note St John's astute comments regarding Jane: 'human affections and sympathies have a most powerful hold on you' (p. 398). He is a good judge of character, as this and the following observations prove.

GLOSSARY   **halcyon** calm and pleasant

Calvinistic form of early Protestantism which opposed the Catholic idea that we could be saved by good works, and believed that our lives were mapped out in advance by God

CHAPTER 31

Although Jane is unhappy she feels she has chosen the right path.

Jane spends her first day as mistress of the school. When it is over she struggles with herself for feeling sad when she should be contented and happy; concern for Rochester plagues her thoughts. She does not regret her decision, however, and knows that she is in some measure being rewarded for acting correctly.

St John visits her and, guessing correctly at the source of her distress, warns against yielding to temptation and always instead attempting to lead a Godly life. Miss Oliver, the beautiful daughter of a wealthy landowner, arrives. Jane immediately spots that St John is completely in love with this girl, who is also apparently infatuated with him.

COMMENT   There is an interesting symmetry in St John's devotion for Miss Oliver, and Jane's for Rochester. Both turn away from the fierce love they feel: both are immensely affected by it but choose not to give it sway.

Jane's admiration for beauty has no sense of envy about it; she can value a beautiful face sincerely, but does not put as much store by physical appearance as good character.

GLOSSARY   **delf** earthenware
                      cypher do arithmetic

CHAPTER 32

Jane values romantic love very highly.

Jane settles in well to her new life, and is soon accepted by the neighbourhood. She finds much to be satisfied with, but is still tormented regularly by dreams of Rochester.

The deep love St John feels for Rosamund Oliver becomes more apparent, as does her affection for him. One evening as Jane is making the finishing touches to a painting of the lady, St John enters and his reaction to the lovely face prompts Jane into a frank discussion with him. She feels that if they were to marry, he could use his fortune in good works just as well as by going abroad as a missionary. He acknowledges his love for the girl, but is determined to stick to his course. He argues that their marriage would not work as they were such different characters, and would tire of each other within a year.

As he is leaving he notices something scribbled on a scrap of Jane's drawing paper which obviously shocks him; he quickly tears it away and leaves hurriedly.

COMMENT   Further exploration of St John's refusal to take the path of love and happiness reveals similarities with Jane, but not so direct as first appeared. He blindly follows the one path of missionary: his zealous religious beliefs dominating all other feeling. Where Jane turned away from love in fear of disgrace and misery, St John chooses to denounce the feeling he has for Rosamund because he has already committed himself to another road in life, whatever the personal cost. His stern nature commands him at all times, even restricting the time he allows Jane to talk of Rosamund to him: '"go on for another quarter of an hour." And he actually took out his watch and laid it upon the table to measure the time' (p. 416).

GLOSSARY   **'It was the 5th of November, and a holiday'** school cancelled for Guy Fawkes's day
Marmion poem by Sir Walter Scott, published 1808

CHAPTER 33

Look at Jane's reaction to the news and what most interests her in St John's narrative (see Literary Terms).

The next night sees the return of St John who has struggled through a severe snowstorm to get to Jane's cottage, clearly on important business. After a period of silent contemplation he narrates to her her own history, proving that he is in full possession of the truth. Although shocked, she is far more concerned with any news of Rochester he may have, and fiercely defends St John's judgement of the former's behaviour.

When she hears that the country has been searched for her because she has been left a fortune of £20,000 by her uncle, she is staggered. When it further transpires that St John, Diana and Mary are her family – first cousins, in fact – she is delighted and immediately insists that the fortune be split four ways: 'it could never be mine in justice, though it might be in law' (p. 431).

COMMENT   The existence of a kind of natural justice, a moral and fair system which can sometimes go against society's legal system, has echoes back to Rochester's appeal to a higher court than that of man to judge his actions. This reinforces the idea that Jane and Rochester have similar ways of viewing the world.

Family is very important to her: remember St John's observation that 'human affections and sympathies have a most powerful hold upon you' (p. 398). She is more excited by the idea that she is now part of a family, having been always a friendless orphan. The refusal to accept the full sum also highlights the aspect of her character which values love, friendship and decency above finance and its trappings.

GLOSSARY   **Medusa** snake-headed monster from Greek myth, who turned to stone any who looked directly at her

CHAPTER 34

Jane is always trying to please those she admires.

Jane works hard to make Moor House ready for the return of Mary and Diana. The three are delighted to see each other again, and life settles down into a warm and happy routine very quickly. St John becomes more distant, however, and appears to be studying Jane much of the time. He asks her to assist him in his study of Hindustanee, a language he needs to master before he goes to India as a missionary. His hold over her becomes more and more pronounced, and she feels a claustrophobic need to please him at all times, as if he is constantly judging her.

MARSH END – ADULTHOOD AND THE ROAD TO KNOWLEDGE

Note how Jane Several months pass. Jane tries to find out what has
still remains firm happened to Rochester, but meets with no success. She
in her ideas about becomes more and more despondent as she waits in
love. vain for news. On one occasion, when she is moved to
tears, St John asks her to take a walk during which he
asks her to come with him as a missionary. She agrees
to this, feeling it futile to stay any longer waiting for
'some impossible change in circumstances' (p. 450)
which might bring her back to the man she loves.
However, St John also wants her to marry him, and this
she cannot agree to, knowing that her idea of love is so
different from his.

COMMENT She comments on the aspect of her nature that always
complies with characters stronger than her own up
to the moment of 'determined revolt' (p. 446). There
are echoes of the confrontations with Mrs Reed and
Rochester in her interview with St John.

Her passionate side which values the beauty of true love
is clearly displayed in her rejection of St John's offer.
She rejects the idea of being 'forced to keep the fire of
my nature continually low, to compel it to burn
inwardly and never utter a cry, though the imprisoned
flame consumed vital after vital (organ)' (p. 453): a
dramatic and moving description of the horror she feels
at living in a loveless marriage.

GLOSSARY   **taciturnity** tendency towards quiet

CHAPTER 35

St John retreats from Jane emotionally: although polite,
he is cold and distant. She feels this deeply and
continually tries to make amends, although she still
refuses absolutely to be his wife. When Mary and
Diana hear of his proposal they are equally determined

that the idea would be terrible and that she should on no account marry him on these terms.

However, his coldness has a marked effect on her. The day before he is to leave, she is so beaten down by his refusal to be her friend that, when he asks her one last time to change her mind she is swayed into accepting. At this very moment, one charged with emotion, she hears Rochester's voice calling her desperately.

COMMENT

Note the similarity in Jane's position here to that of Chapter 27 when Rochester pleads with her. Again she is placed in a difficult dilemma and is tempted in spite of her better judgement.

Think how the similarity of situations increases the poignancy of Jane's dilemma.

The moving poetry of this last section of the chapter is very dramatic, calculated to draw the reader into the emotion of the events and participate in the sense of climax to the story. Much has been written of the experience that Jane and Rochester share, that of 'hearing' each other over a long distance. She asks us to judge for ourselves, and one explanation could be that they share an extreme emotion at the same moment which somehow enables them to communicate with each other. To dissect this rather than accept it is to undermine the force of this part of the **narrative** (see Literary Terms). The idea of spiritual communication reinforces the notion of a 'sympathy' between them.

GLOSSARY

Revelations fiery part of the Old Testament, full of punishment for wrongdoing
hierophant high priest, religious leader

Identify the speaker.

1 'Why do I struggle to retain a valueless life?'

5 'I am cold: no fervour infects me'

2 'my heart rather warms to the poor little soul'

4 'I am sure you cannot long be content to pass your leisure in solitude'

3 'If you are a Christian, you ought not to consider poverty a crime'

Identify the person 'to whom' this comment refers.

6 'You tremble and become flushed whenever Miss Oliver enters the school-room'

7 'She is well named the Rose of the World, indeed!'

8 'you are docile, diligent, disinterested, faithful, constant, and courageous'

Check your answers on page 90.

 Consider these issues.

a The effects of the use of **imagery** (see Literary Terms) of marble and stone in the descriptions of St John.

b What lessons Jane learns about the nature of poverty when she is forced to endure it herself.

c Notice the use of 'colloquial' English to denote persons of a lower social class.

d How Jane's excitement at having a home of her own is reflected in cleaning and decorating Moor House.

e St John is accurate in some of his opinions of Jane's nature, but does he appreciate the whole essence of her as well as Rochester does?

CHAPTERS 36–38: CONCLUSION – THE JOURNEY HOME

CHAPTER 36

Note the way in which we can see that Jane is now a confident adult.

Now bent on a purpose which directs her every move, Jane prepares to return to Thornfield to ascertain once and for all what has happened to Rochester. She takes another journey in the same coach which carried her to Marsh End a year before. After making some enquiries, she walks to Thornfield and is shocked and dismayed to find it a 'blackened ruin'.

Hurrying back to the inn, she hears from the owner that Mrs Rochester had started a fire in Jane's bed before throwing herself from the battlements. Rochester, who had become distraught after Jane's disappearance, saves the servants and tries to help his wife, but is blinded and loses an arm in the process. The innkeeper tells her that he now lives alone at Ferndean Manor; she prepares to go there immediately.

COMMENT   Hearing her own story from the point of view of a disinterested observer is uncomfortable to Jane but interesting to us, as Rochester's deep love for her is reinforced by the tale of his behaviour after her disappearance. Also, his actions in the fire are admirable and go a long way to validating him as a good and noble man in our eyes, whereas before we may have been judging him harshly. However, Jane's sense and judgement have been so constantly and completely reinforced that by this stage in the **narrative** (see Literary Terms) we can have little doubt that if she loves him so completely, he must be worthy of that love.

GLOSSARY   **door-stones** doorstep

CONCLUSION – THE JOURNEY HOME

CHAPTER 37

Jane still teases Rochester and keeps him at a distance for a while.

Jane's first sight of Rochester evokes pain and pity; he is a changed man, scarred both physically and emotionally by the events of the past year. She watches him for a while in secrecy, then announces herself at the house and surprises him in his living room. He cannot believe it is her: so many times has he dreamt of her return that he feels she is still a figment of his imagination.

The next day is spent blissfully getting to know one another again. He questions her closely about her whereabouts, and shows some jealousy of St John. She puts his mind at rest on that score, and when he repeats his proposal to her, she accepts without hesitation. He shows a great deal of remorse for his past actions and pride, and feels that God has inflicted a just series of punishments on him from which he has learned humility and repentance. When he thanks God for his fate and promises to 'lead henceforth a purer life than I have done hitherto!' (p. 497), we can rest assured that his life with Jane will be a happy one; that they both deserve and have earned contentment.

Comment   Jane's qualities and talents have always been
undervalued, hidden to all except herself, the reader,
and the few who deserve to appreciate them. They are
less important in society's eyes than beauty, grace,
money and social status. Therefore in her society she
has always been unequal to those with whom she
associates. Now, however, she is on equal status with
Rochester: financially, physically and emotionally. This
is very important to the future success of their
relationship: note how uncomfortable she was with the
engagement gifts he tried to heap on her, and how he
now comments **ironically** (see Literary Terms): 'Never
mind fine clothes and jewels, now: all that is not worth
a fillip' (p. 495). Where once she was dependent upon
him, they are now the same in every way.

GLOSSARY   **grass-plat** lawn
blent blended
'only lonely
cicatrized visage scarred face
brownie helpful household elf, i.e., the story of the 'Elves and
Shoemaker'

CHAPTER 38

*Look for other
examples in the
text where
moments of high
emotion are
glossed over with
the minimum of
words.*

The announcement of the wedding is made very simply
and Jane and Rochester are married, quietly, without
fuss, within the three days he promised. The final
chapter calmly and simply describes their life together
as one of sheer contentment and bliss: of a couple
perfectly suited to each other in every respect.

The very last part of Jane's narration fills in details of
the ten years that have passed. Adèle is placed in a good
school by Jane, and grows into a fine young woman.
Diana and Mary both marry good men and lead happy
lives. Rochester regains the sight of his one eye, and is
thus able to see his baby boy when he is born.

The story ends with St John Rivers: tireless devotion to his mission has weakened his health and Jane awaits news of his death, but does not weep for this. She knows that he is perfectly contented and joyous at the prospect of meeting his Maker.

COMMENT   The words 'Reader, I married him' (p. 498) are often assumed to be the final ones of the novel, and tend to overshadow the paragraphs about St John, which have significant status at the end of the story. This reinforces Christianity as one of the very important **themes** (see Literary Terms) in the book, and makes it a book about religion as much as about romantic love.

GLOSSARY   **cadet of the house** male child
oculist eye doctor

A   *Identify the speaker.*

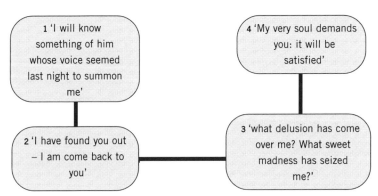

1 'I will know something of him whose voice seemed last night to summon me'

4 'My very soul demands you: it will be satisfied'

2 'I have found you out – I am come back to you'

3 'what delusion has come over me? What sweet madness has seized me?'

Identify the person 'to whom' this comment refers.

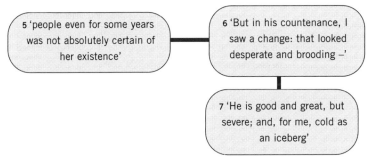

5 'people even for some years was not absolutely certain of her existence'

6 'But in his countenance, I saw a change: that looked desperate and brooding –'

7 'He is good and great, but severe; and, for me, cold as an iceberg'

Check your answers on page 90.

B   *Consider these issues.*

a How Jane has much more authority and command of situations in this section.

b The pleasure in their lives together is surrounded by nature rather than rich trappings.

c Whether Rochester is 'rewarded' by the return of his sight for leading a better life.

d The fact that Jane announces her own wedding, putting her in control of her life.

PART THREE

COMMENTARY

THEMES

Although several of the major **themes** (see Literary Terms) are discussed below, they are by no means a definitive list and it would be useful for you to consider how many others there are. It is often difficult to think about a theme in isolation and you will probably find that strands of a theme tend to overlap with each other.

ROMANCE

Jane Eyre is of course a love story and the relationship between her and Rochester is the main focus of the plot. On the surface Charlotte Brontë is making use of a very simple plot line which is familiar throughout the history of storytelling: boy meets girl, boy loses girl, boy and girl are reunited after some hardship and they all live happily ever after. This plot recurs again and again throughout all cultures and times.

This is an important idea that internal beauty is more important than external.

Jane and Rochester are both passionate characters who have an enormous capacity to love. Neither one of them is physically attractive which is important because beauty often deflects attention away from character, which it must not do in their case. They are clearly well suited, but have to be separated in order to experience an individual time of character development before they can finally enjoy peace together. Jane needs to become Rochester's equal in independence and maturity: her physical struggle and emotional torment strengthen her character and turn her into a woman rather than a naïve girl. Rochester has committed a selfless act and proves that he has seen the error of his former ways in order to become a whole person again, now needing her as much as she needs him. **Ironically** (see Literary Terms), he is a better man without his sight and his arm than when he was whole, and Jane loves him better for being vulnerable than when he was fiercely independent. The nature of true love and marriage is examined in other relationships in the book:

- Aunt Reed's refusal to keep the promise made to her dead husband
- the scornful description of cousin Georgiana's 'advantageous match' (p. 272)
- the prospect of a union between Rochester and Blanche Ingram, clearly good financially and socially, but not true love
- St John Rivers's love for Rosamund Oliver which is described as possibly a surface attraction: 'While something in me … is acutely sensible to her charms, something else is as deeply impressed with her defects' (p. 417)
- the prospect of a marriage of duty and convenience between Jane and St John, passionately rejected by the former: 'I scorn your idea of love, I scorn the counterfeit sentiment you offer' (p. 454)

RELIGION

The nature of Christianity is explored in great detail throughout the novel, so much so that many people say it is as much a book about religion as it is a love story. Jane's system of value judgement is founded on a strict moral code. Think about examples in the text where she displays the following attributes:

- putting others before herself and not being judgemental
- valuing good character more highly than surface appearance
- working hard to deserve the good opinion of others

There are several very 'religious' people in the novel. It is interesting to note Jane's reaction to each of them, and that whilst she can admire some and condemn others, she adheres to her own system of belief throughout. Think about her reaction to the following:

- Helen Burns, who displays the doctrine of 'turning the other cheek' constantly. She suffers terribly and never complains, even when unfairly treated
- Mr Brocklehurst, who is fearsome and tyrannical, and uses religion as a justification for cruelty and neglect

Note the irony in the comment that Eliza endowed the convent with her fortune.

- Eliza Reed, a cold and fervent woman who gives her life to God by joining a nunnery. Jane views this with detached cynicism: 'You are not without sense, cousin Eliza; but what you have, I suppose in another year will be walled up alive in a French convent' (p. 273)
- St John Rivers, a passionately religious man who is on a quest for the best way to give his life to God

In the end Jane chooses to believe that she is entitled to lead a happy life and that in doing so she can still serve God: 'if ever I thought a good thought – if ever I prayed a sincere and blameless prayer – if ever I wished a righteous wish, – I am rewarded now. To be your wife is, for me, to be as happy as I can be on earth' (p. 494). She chooses a path similar to Miss Temple, Diana and Mary Rivers, which reinforces the rightness of her decision.

FEMALE INDEPENDENCE

This novel is often said to be a very political book because it explores the idea of a woman alone, in charge of her own life and making her own decisions. Jane could easily be described as a 'feminist'. She rejects the man she loves until such time as she can be his equal. She would rather be alone and independent than with Rochester on his terms (see p. 402).

Miss Temple, Diana and Mary Rivers all possess the values Jane admires. They all have to work for a living, and are therefore financially dependent on others. They all marry for love men who deserve them, rather than settling for financial security at the expense of happiness. Jane is very conscious that these women are not treated as they deserve to be: note the description of Miss Temple's reaction to being admonished by Mr Brocklehurst – 'she now gazed straight before her, and her face, actually pale as marble, appeared to be assuming also the coldness and fixity of that material' (p. 75). She hates the thought of Diana and Mary wasting their talents as governesses: 'by whose wealthy and haughty members they were regarded only as humble dependents, and who neither knew nor sought one of their innate excellences' (p. 394). It is just as important for the novel to end comfortably by them finding happiness in an equal relationship.

Jane also suffers years of female subservience.

Throughout her life Jane is placed in situations where she is dependent on others. She learns to keep her passionate and assertive side quiet except when driven to extremes: 'I never in my life have known any medium in my dealings with positive, hard characters, antagonistic to my own, between absolute submission and determined revolt' (p. 446). Look again at three episodes which denote this clearly: her outburst towards Mrs Reed (pp. 45–6), her refusal of Rochester in Chapter 27 and her refusal of St John during Chapters 34–5.

Nonetheless, she is an assertive heroine. Look at the confidence and eloquence in her **dialogues** (see Literary Terms) with Rochester from the start of their relationship. She is neither meek nor subservient with anyone; she often chooses to keep quiet rather than speak her mind unguardedly, but when called upon she is forthright and powerfully honest in her opinions.

Examine how Bertha is described by Jane. Look for the hints that show her to be a victim rather than an aggressor.

This **theme** (see Literary Terms) would not be complete without mention of the other strong female presence of the novel: Bertha Rochester. For a different perspective on her story it is worth considering the ideas in *The Wide Sargasso Sea* by Jean Rhys (see Broader Perspectives). Many feminist interpretations of Jane Eyre have leapt to the defence of Bertha and used her to pronounce harsh judgement on Rochester. We never know if his account of their marriage and early years is true; we are given but one side of the story and there are several clues which help us begin to form a clearer judgement of the situation (see Characters, on Bertha).

- Rochester views her as a malignant presence and uses devilish **imagery** (see Literary Terms) in his descriptions of her.
- She never, however, attempts to harm anyone apart from him and herself, in spite of the opportunities she has to attack Jane.
- Her brother speaks of her with tenderness: 'Let her be taken care of; let her be treated as tenderly as may be' (p. 242).

SOCIAL STATUS

Think about why this idea is relevant to Jane and her situation.

The existence of a strict and rigid class system is often referred to. Money is a guiding factor to where one fits on the social ladder. The **theme** (see Literary Terms) of respect being earned and not deserved due to one's bank balance is important.

In general, the characters seem to divide fairly easily into two categories – the rich landed gentry and the dependent classes who have to work to earn money. Think about the following in particular:
Miss Ingram
Rosamund Oliver

Mrs Reed
Miss Temple
Diana and Mary Rivers
Mrs Fairfax
Georgiana Reed
Jane
Rochester
St John Rivers

A useful exercise would be to find descriptions of each of these characters, and see if the rich are more or less admired than the dependent. It appears that Jane attaches very little value to wealth and does not see it as the road to any kind of happy life: look at her reaction to the prospect of owning a fortune on p. 432.

Think whether Jane's attitude towards money would be any different if she herself were wealthy.

Although Jane is not rich she has been brought up to be ladylike and is therefore very different to the working-class farming people she associates with at Marsh End. Think about your reaction to her description of them on p. 401: 'Some of them are unmannered, rough, intractable, as well as ignorant; … I must not forget that these coarsely clad little peasants are of flesh and blood as good as the scions of gentlest genealogy.' To us this can sound quite patronising, but remember that social status was fixed and people from one class mixed rarely with those of another, so Jane would be shocked at what she found.

Another example of the rigidity of social class is in the reaction to her parents' marriage: her mother was cast off for marrying someone from an 'inferior' class to herself. These societal forms and conventions were strictly adhered to in the nineteenth century.

The autobiographical form of *Jane Eyre* means that the novel follows a **linear, chronological narrative** (see Literary Terms). The idea of a journey through life is strongly highlighted by the five significant journeys that Jane takes. Her personal journey has several purposes:

- from childhood to maturity
- bondage to freedom
- unhappiness to happiness
- innocence to knowledge

Jane goes though severe tests at each stage: almost rites of passage, so that she can eventually deserve her happiness.

Each phase of Jane's development is marked by a solitary journey. It is only when she reaches her destination that the journey is at an end – which is marked by her settling at Ferndean Manor for life.

There are five general 'sections' to the novel: Jane's childhood at Gateshead; her school years; time at Thornfield; Marsh End; and the conclusion or 'happy ending'. Although the novel covers the whole of Jane's life, only the most dramatic two years are dwelt upon in detail. The Thornfield section is the longest in spite of being the shortest period of time: seventeen chapters out of a total thirty-eight are devoted to this period. This marks it as the most important phase of Jane's life, as well as the most interesting to the reader.

JANE

Jane Eyre is the **eponymous** (see Literary Terms) heroine of the novel. Strong willed and passionate, her search for true love and happiness forms the story of the novel. She has a well-developed sense of right and wrong from an early age. She is a very good judge of character as a child, warming instantly to Miss Temple and Helen Burns, whilst loathing Mrs Reed and Mr Brocklehurst.

Small but strong willed

Financially dependent but independent of spirit

Shy but passionate

Her strong personal integrity is a marked feature of her personality. She is aware that she is penniless and alone in the world and has to be very independent. She may be naïve and innocent but she is able to look after herself very well. Twice in her life she has to make very difficult choices, one to leave Mr Rochester and the other to reject St John Rivers. On both these occasions she is faced with very strong-willed characters, but she masters both of them and has her own way. People are of paramount importance to her but she retains her independence of mind in spite of her need to be accepted and loved. Her search is for unconditional acceptance, and she sacrifices nothing of herself in her relationships with others.

There is a passionate woman hidden underneath Jane's shy and deferential appearance. She is deeply religious, and her faith in God is at times the only thing which sustains her. However, she refuses to accept the belief of Helen Burns and St John Rivers that she should sacrifice happiness on earth in order to get to Heaven. She wants happiness now, and eventually gets everything she deserves.

Mr Rochester

Romantic and arrogant
Lonely and passionate
Immoral and responsible

Mr Rochester is a fascinating, romantic figure. He is a very unhappy man when we first meet him. At a very young age his father and elder brother tricked him into his marriage with Bertha Mason in order that he should get her dowry of £30,000. When he discovers that she is insane he has to bear the responsibility of this alone, and only brings her to Thornfield Hall when his brother dies and the house is left to him. He then runs away abroad to try to forget his troubles by leading an immoral life, but the knowledge of Bertha's existence haunts him and his shady life only helps to turn him bitter.

His pure love for Jane eventually changes him back to the man he was, but his actions towards her have often been judged very harshly. He does attempt to marry her illegally, but we feel such sympathy for his predicament and his immense love for Jane that his actions can be understood. He is a man who believes he is doing the best he can for his mad wife, although locking a woman in one windowless room for ten years with a drunkard for a keeper is a questionable way of doing the right thing.

He redeems himself by his actions in the fire which destroys Thornfield, as well as by appreciating and loving Jane. He is only allowed contentment after he has suffered and recognised 'the error of his ways': 'I began to see and acknowledge the hand of God in my doom. I began to experience remorse, repentance; the wish for reconcilement to my Maker' (p. 495). His blinded and crippled state is a **metaphor** (see Literary Terms) for his loss of arrogance and pride. We feel that he is now worthy of the love Jane feels for him, and indeed it would have been difficult for her to be equally matched with someone less passionate and forceful than herself.

BERTHA

Insane and cunning

Hidden yet ever-present

The first Mrs Rochester, or 'the madwoman in the attic', is an intriguing subject. She is an elusive figure who never speaks and is only seen twice, and yet she dominates the central action of the novel. Her presence is felt powerfully from the moment Jane enters Thornfield: 'It was a curious laugh; distinct, formal, mirthless' (p. 122).

Her actions are dramatic and violent, and very interesting to interpret. She attacks Rochester twice, once by attempting to burn his bed, and second by flying at him when he presents her to Jane and the others. She attacks her brother when he comes to visit her. She tears Jane's wedding veil the night before her marriage. And her final act before her suicide is to set fire to Jane's bed.

We have to accept that she is believed to be insane because that is what we are told. Rochester is vague on the subject of her illness and makes the problem sound more like a difference in character and temperament than insanity. Moreover, her actions do seem to suggest that she is aware of what is going on at Thornfield, which makes us wonder what kind of insanity she is suffering from. Could she be a woman driven to madness by an unsympathetic husband? There is an implicit jealousy of Jane in her actions, or at least her position as recipient of Rochester's love. She manifests great anger towards her husband: maybe because she loves him, or because he has kept her shut away for so long. However we choose to interpret her character and motives, she is not to be ignored as a side-issue in the novel.

ST JOHN

St John Rivers is a religious fanatic. He is young and handsome, very intelligent and well-educated. His religious conviction goes beyond that of all his close associates, including his sisters and Jane, and becomes the dominant force of his personality.

*Fanatical and
cold
Inflexible and
altruistic*

During the nineteenth century many deeply religious people went to third-world countries to bring Christianity to the 'heathens'. It was from this source that much of the world was converted to Christianity. It seems quite an arrogant idea to place Christianity above any other religion, but it is important to remember that people such as St John were convinced that you could only be 'saved' if you were a Christian.

The problem with St John is that his beliefs are so profound and inflexible that he allows for no human faults, and this makes him an austere character. Jane clearly struggles with this aspect of him, because she can see his kindness in his devotion to helping others no matter what the personal sacrifice. Jane believes that she can serve God by enjoying the life that He gave her, whereas St John believes that the only way to ensure a place in Heaven is to devote your life to others at the expense of your own comfort and happiness.

MINOR CHARACTERS

Mrs Reed

Jane's aunt Reed is her guardian. Jane spends ten unhappy years in her house with her three objectionable children, John, Eliza and Georgiana. Mrs Reed is clearly a stern and cold woman who has no feelings for Jane at all and makes no effort to get along with her, in spite of promises made to her dead husband to raise her as a daughter.

Jane sees being sent to school by Mrs Reed as a victory; whereas for Mrs Reed it tastes of punishment.

She is evidently relieved to ship Jane off to school, and makes no further contact with her until Jane is an adult and Mrs Reed is on her deathbed. She hates Jane so much that she tells Jane's uncle she is dead rather than give her whereabouts. Family disgrace and financial ruin seem to be fitting punishments for so cruel a woman, but Jane forgives her. In spite of being close to death she refuses to be reconciled with Jane, indeed managing to blame her for the dreadful act: 'You were born, I think, to be my torment: my last hour is racked by the recollection of a deed, which, but for you, I should never have been tempted to commit' (p. 268). Her function in the novel is important for two reasons: little Jane is able to show how she responds to senseless cruelty, and the adult Jane is able to demonstrate her lack of vindictiveness: 'I long earnestly to be reconciled to you now: kiss me, aunt' (p. 269).

Helen

Helen Burns is another pupil at Lowood school. Jane is instantly drawn to her when she arrives there. Helen's illness is announced before we even meet her: 'the sound of a cough close behind me, made me turn my head'. She is to have a profound effect on Jane's life in many ways. She is the first person ever to be consistently kind to Jane – her first friend, in fact. She is clearly very intelligent and well read: qualities Jane admires very much as they lead to independence of mind.

She is a Christian in the true sense of the word. She believes that it is her duty to suffer patiently whatever punishment she is given. Jane reacts strongly to this: 'I could not comprehend this doctrine of endurance' (p. 66).

Jane does not know that Helen is very ill, although her coughing would have alerted the contemporary reader to the fact that she has tuberculosis, a common disease at that time. Her death affects Jane so profoundly that she never mentions her again, although we know that she visits her grave fifteen years later and erects the gravestone in her memory. Helen's function is to give Jane a friend and ally at Lowood, and to introduce the ideas of religious sacrifice which run through the novel.

Miss Temple
As superintendent of Lowood School, Miss Temple is Jane's teacher for six years and friend for two, serving as a role model in many respects: 'to her instruction I owed the best part of my acquirements; her friendship and society had been my continual solace; she had stood me in the stead of mother, governess, and latterly, companion' (p. 98). She is clearly a very good teacher, knowledgeable and intelligent as well as kind and fair. Her effect is so strong that when she leaves Lowood to be married Jane feels the loss of 'the serene atmosphere I had been breathing in her vicinity' (p. 99).

She stands up to Mr Brocklehurst and defends the girls against his strict regime. He is a fearsome man as well as her superior, and yet she is not afraid to defend the children when she feels he is inflicting too much unnecessary suffering.

Mr Brocklehurst
The clergyman in charge of Lowood, Mr Brocklehurst is Jane's first experience of a religious person. He is harsh and austere, and uses religion as a justification for treating the girls at Lowood cruelly. He is a hypocrite however, because although he advocates physical suffering for the girls, his wife and daughters are allowed to wear fancy clothes and rich jewels. His regime is partially to blame for so many of the girls dying of typhus fever, and there is a strong sense of relief when his charge of the school is taken away from him.

He is clearly an acquaintance of Mrs Reed; this is a strong indicator that he is not a pleasant man, because we already know enough of her character to assume that anyone she admires will not be a nice person.

Mrs Fairfax

Placid and kind

Alice Fairfax is the matronly housekeeper of Thornfield Hall. She is a distant relation of the Rochesters and a trusted employee. She has a great deal of common sense, and Jane respects her very much. She is Jane's second mother figure (after Miss Temple) and Jane admires her discretion as well as occasionally despairing of it.

She is somewhat baffled by Rochester's relationship with Jane, and is very concerned about the proposed marriage. Although this is never made clear, it is possible that she knows the real identity of 'the madwoman in the attic', and this is why she warns Jane to take care. Jane is uncomfortable with this warning but it is meant kindly and has much truth in it.

Grace Poole

Mrs Poole is a servant, hired to keep charge of Bertha. Her presence at Thornfield Hall is used to explain the strange noises and events that Jane witnesses. She appears contented in her strange, isolated occupation.

Grace drinks too much; Rochester refers to her 'temporary lapses' by which he means alcoholic stupors. This is possibly excusable, given the circumstances of her life. She has developed a close relationship with her charge and understands her very well.

Diana and Mary Rivers

The sisters of St John are to become Jane's sisters in mind if not in blood tie, although it transpires that they are related. They are very similar to Jane: educated, interesting, kind and gentle. Jane blossoms in their company, becoming more relaxed and confident because she is liked and respected by those whom she likes and respects. They have a significant function in aiding Jane to reach maturity and complete her sense of self.

Miss Ingram

Beautiful and self-possessed

Arrogant and malicious

Blanche Ingram is everything that Jane is not: of a titled, wealthy family, majestic and beautiful, self-confident and with all the social graces: she appears to be the perfect match for Mr Rochester, or so poor Jane thinks, and Mr Rochester teasingly allows her and us readers to continue to believe this, thus making Jane's love for him appear all the more poignant, and keeping us readers in suspense. However, though Blanche may have a superficial cleverness, she is also arrogant, vain and with a touch of malice. She is no match, in Mr Rochester's eyes, for Jane's intellect, modesty and pragmatism; indeed, she is not to Mr Rochester's taste at all. She is as loud and brash as Jane is deferential. In many ways they are polar opposites of each other.

LANGUAGE & STYLE

The facsimile of the frontispiece to the first edition of this novel describes it: '*Jane Eyre*: an Autobiography, edited by Currer Bell'. The book is not, however, an autobiography but a work of fiction. And of course Jane Eyre is not a real person, but a character existing in a **narrative** (see Literary Terms). However, the novel is highly reminiscent of an autobiography. It is narrated in the first person, thereby immediately drawing the reader into a closer sense of identification with the central character, and implicitly creating more of a sense of realism. Also, as twentieth-century readers, we have knowledge about the author unknown to the contemporary readership. We know that many details of the work were drawn directly from the author's personal experience. Many characters, situations, and places are taken from her own life. And the **eponymous** (see Literary Terms) heroine bears, in many respects, a startling resemblance to Charlotte Brontë herself. Although not completely autobiographical, this novel is not completely fictional either.

The use of this technique allows the reader a more empathic response.

Jane constantly addresses her 'reader' directly: 'Reader, I married him' (p. 498). This draws attention to the fact that there is a **narrator** (see Literary Terms) here telling a story, but we are invited to believe it is real: 'whether what followed was the effect of excitement, the reader shall judge' (p. 466). To a certain extent Brontë was following literary convention by exploring the use of **narrative** stance in story telling. For example, she often shifts between past and **present tense** (see Literary Terms) for different effects. Her heroine is not an **omniscient narrator** (see Literary Terms); therefore, the reader is able to see things that Jane cannot, and participate in the story: we have an overview which she doesn't share.

The language of the novel is very difficult to someone unfamiliar with nineteenth-century texts. The sentences are long and complicated, and the vocabulary is elaborate. This formal **prose** (see Literary Terms) was very common at this time, in spoken and written language. However, the very nature of some of the language highlights that Jane is an articulate, intelligent woman, whose language reflects her learning.

PART FOUR

STUDY SKILLS

HOW TO USE QUOTATIONS

One of the secrets of success in writing essays is the way you use quotations. There are five basic principles:

- Put inverted commas at the beginning and end of the quotation
- Write the quotation exactly as it appears in the original
- Do not use a quotation that repeats what you have just written
- Use the quotation so that it fits into your sentence
- Keep the quotation as short as possible

Quotations should be used to develop the line of thought in your essays.

Your comment should not duplicate what is in your quotation. For example:

> Jane is devastated at the idea of having to leave Thornfield: 'I see the necessity of departure; and it is like looking on the necessity of death.'

Far more effective is to write:

> Jane sees how important it is for her to leave Thornfield, although it feels like 'the necessity of death'.

The most sophisticated way of using the writer's words is to embed them into your sentence:

> Jane is struck 'with terror and anguish' at the idea of leaving Thornfield for ever.

When you use quotations in this way, you are demonstrating the ability to use text as evidence to support your ideas - not simply including words from the original to prove you have read it.

Everyone writes differently. Work through the suggestions given here and adapt the advice to suit your own style and interests. This will improve your essay-writing skills and allow your personal voice to emerge.

The following points indicate in ascending order the skills of essay writing:

- Picking out one or two facts about the story and adding the odd detail
- Writing about the text by retelling the story
- Retelling the story and adding a quotation here and there
- Organising an answer which explains what is happening in the text and giving quotations to support what you write

....

- Writing in such a way as to show that you have thought about the intentions of the writer of the text and that you understand the techniques used
- Writing at some length, giving your viewpoint on the text and commenting by picking out details to support your views
- Looking at the text as a work of art, demonstrating clear critical judgement and explaining to the reader of your essay how the enjoyment of the text is assisted by literary devices, linguistic effects and psychological insights; showing how the text relates to the time when it was written

The dotted line above represents the division between lower- and higher-level grades. Higher-level performance begins when you start to consider your response as a reader of the text. The highest level is reached when you offer an enthusiastic personal response and show how this piece of literature is a product of its time.

Coursework essay

Set aside an hour or so at the start of your work to plan what you have to do.

- List all the points you feel are needed to cover the task. Collect page references of information and quotations that will support what you have to say. A helpful tool is the highlighter pen: this saves painstaking copying and enables you to target precisely what you want to use.
- Focus on what you consider to be the main points of the essay. Try to sum up your argument in a single sentence, which could be the closing sentence of your essay. Depending on the essay title, it could be a statement about a character: The essence of Jane's character is that she retains her independence of spirit and triumphs over repression and cruelty; an opinion about setting: The author continually emphasises mood and theme by stressing the importance of external surroundings; or a judgement on a theme: *Jane Eyre* remains a fascinating and popular novel because the theme of romantic love is just as relevant today as it has ever been.
- Make a short essay plan. Use the first paragraph to introduce the argument you wish to make. In the following paragraphs develop this argument with details, examples and other possible points of view. Sum up your argument in the last paragraph. Check you have answered the question.
- Write the essay, remembering all the time the central point you are making.
- On completion, go back over what you have written to eliminate careless errors and improve expression. Read it aloud to yourself, or, if you are feeling more confident, to a relative or friend.

If you can, try to type your essay using a word processor. This will allow you to correct and improve your writing without spoiling its appearance.

Examination essay

The essay written in an examination often carries more marks than the coursework essay even though it is written under considerable time pressure.

In the revision period build up notes on various aspects of the text you are using. Fortunately, in acquiring this set of York Notes on *Jane Eyre*, you have made a prudent beginning! York Notes are set out to give you vital information and help you to construct your personal overview of the text.

Make notes with appropriate quotations about the key issues of the set text. Go into the examination knowing your text and having a clear set of opinions about it.

In most English Literature examinations you can take in copies of your set books. This is an enormous advantage although it may lull you into a false sense of security. Beware! There is simply not enough time in an examination to read the book from scratch.

In the examination

- Read the question paper carefully and remind yourself what you have to do.
- Look at the questions on your set texts to select the one that most interests you and mentally work out the points you wish to stress.
- Remind yourself of the time available and how you are going to use it.
- Briefly map out a short plan in note form that will keep your writing on track and illustrate the key argument you want to make.
- Then set about writing it.
- When you have finished, check through to eliminate errors.

To summarise, these are keys to success

- **Know the text**
- **Have a clear understanding of and opinions on the storyline, characters, setting, themes and writer's concerns**
- **Select the right material**
- **Plan and write a clear response, continually bearing the question in mind**

The following essay plan will show you how to structure an essay and will provide you with some ideas on the following title. It is divided into six parts and the points below have been made in note form. This is only one possible plan. You may well have your own ideas.

In what ways is the idea of 'journey' significant to the understanding of *Jane Eyre*?

Part 1 Introduce your essay with a general discussion of the five actual journeys that Jane makes during the book, and also introduce the idea that the whole novel is a journey through life for her from childhood innocence to adult maturity.

Part 2 Look in more detail at each of the journeys:
- from Gateshead to Lowood
- from Lowood to Thornfield
- Gateshead to Thornfield
- Thornfield to Marsh End
- Marsh End to Thornfield

Discuss the elements of each – happy or unhappy – what mood she is in, looking forward or back, aware of what she is journeying towards or going into the unknown, etc. Examine the ways in which she is shown to be less vulnerable every time she makes a journey.

Part 3 Now look at the 'figurative' journey in the book. Think about:
- childhood to adulthood
- innocence to maturity
- unhappiness to happiness
- servitude to freedom

Part 4 Conclude by bringing the two ideas together in a paragraph which summarises the ideas, and commenting on the way the literal journeys highlight the central idea of the whole book being a journey. You could mention something about Jane finally reaching her 'destination' in Chapter 38, which is why she writes in the **present tense** (see Literary Terms) rather than looking back into the past.

FURTHER QUESTIONS

1 How are the ideas about 'home' and 'belonging' shown to be important in the story of *Jane Eyre*?

2 Look at Jane's attitude towards Adèle Varens, Blanche Ingram and Diana and Mary Rivers. How do her responses to these characters affect our understanding of her?

3 Discuss the use of weather in the text, with reference to at least three specific occasions.

4 How does Jane's attitude to Gateshead, Thornfield and Moor House highlight her feelings about wealth?

5 Look again at the development of the relationship between Jane and Rochester. What is it that makes her fall in love with him?

6 Re-read the passages in Chapters 15 and 27 where Rochester tells Jane about his early life. What judgements are we being asked to make about his character from this information?

7 How are ideas about religion examined through the characters of Mr Brocklehurst, Eliza Reed and St John Rivers?

8 Carefully reread the information about Bertha Rochester in Chapters 26, 27 and 37. Why might Rochester's viewpoint be different to that of the reader?

9 How do Jane's childhood experiences at Gateshead and Lowood help to form her character?

10 Discuss the theme of romantic love in *Jane Eyre*. Illustrate your answer with reference to her rejection of St John Rivers and acceptance of Rochester.

11 Discuss Charlotte Brontë's attitude to the values of beauty and inner strength of character, looking particularly at her attitude to Blanche Ingram, Rosamund Oliver, Diana and Mary Rivers.

Part five

Cultural connections

Broader perspectives

Film and video versions

Many film and television adaptations have been made of *Jane Eyre* over the years. These are useful because they can increase your understanding of the story, the setting and the characters, although always remember that a film of a book is never as good as the original. Try to keep in mind that you are watching someone else's interpretation of characters and events, and that you might have different opinions. Because the book is very long, all directors have to edit some scenes out. This is an interesting idea because it poses lots of questions about which are vital scenes and which can be removed without destroying the essence of the story.

The most recent film adaptation is directed by Franco Zeffirelli and stars William Hurt and Charlotte Gainsbourg and was released in 1996. This is an excellent version which pays close attention to the importance of setting in the story.

There is also a very gloomy version filmed in 1944 and starring Orson Welles and Joan Fontaine, which is very dark and threatening and clearly recognises what setting adds to the story.

Suggestions for further reading

If you enjoyed *Jane Eyre*, you might like other books by Charlotte Brontë; *Shirley* and *Villette* are the most widely known although neither are as immediately engaging as *Jane Eyre*.

*Wuthering Height*s, by Charlotte's sister Emily, is another powerful and very dramatic love story.

Try reading *The Wide Sargasso Sea* by Jean Rhys, available in Penguin. This is the story of Bertha Rochester and is told partly from her point of view and partly from the young Rochester's, and gives a very interesting slant on the story of *Jane Eyre*.

atmosphere mood – sometimes external, sometimes internal

chronological a style of narrative where the events are ordered in time sequence

dialect regional variations in the use of Standard English

dialogue the speech or conversation of characters

eponymous the person whose name is used as the title of the book

genre a 'kind' or 'type' of literature

Gothic a story of cruel passions and supernatural terrors usually in a medieval setting

image mental picture created with words

imagery figurative language including metaphors and similes

irony the use of words to convey the opposite of their literal meaning; incongruity between what might be expected and what actually occurs

linear similar to chronological – following a straightforward sequence of events

metaphor a descriptive device which states that one thing is another, figuratively rather than literally

narrative the story

narrator the person telling the story, maybe involved or impartial to the story

omniscient literally all-knowing – a type of narrator who knows more about the story than the characters

pathetic fallacy a way of emphasising mood by linking it to the surrounding world

pathos moments which evoke strong feelings of pity or sadness

present tense writing as if experiencing events at that very moment

prose writing not in verse or any other kind of structure

subtext the situation that lies behind the characters or events which may never be directly referred to

theme the central ideas of the novel rather than merely the plot

TEST ANSWERS

TEST YOURSELF (Chapters 1–4)

A 1 Mrs Reed *(Chapter 1)*
2 Mr Lloyd *(Chapter 3)*
3 Jane *(Chapter 4)*
4 Mr Brocklehurst *(Chapter 4)*
5 Jane *(Chapter 3)*
6 Mr Brocklehurst *(Chapter 4)*
7 Jane *(Chapter 3)*

TEST YOURSELF (Chapters 5–10)

A 1 Miss Temple *(Chapter 5)*
2 Helen Burns *(Chapter 5)*
3 Helen Burns *(Chapter 6)*
4 Mr Brocklehurst *(Chapter 7)*
5 Bessie Leaven *(Chapter 5)*
6 Helen Burns *(Chapter 6)*
7 Miss Temple *(Chapter 6)*
8 Jane *(Chapter 7)*

TEST YOURSELF (Chapters 11–27)

A 1 Mrs Fairfax *(Chapter 11)*
2 Mr Rochester *(Chapter 12)*
3 Mr Rochester *(Chapter 14)*
4 Blanche Ingram *(Chapter 17)*
5 Mr Rochester *(Chapter 15)*
6 Jane *(Chapter 23)*
7 Mr Rochester *(Chapter 13)*
8 Blanche Ingram *(Chapter 18)*
9 Bertha Rochester *(Chapter 26)*

TEST YOURSELF (Chapters 28–35)

A 1 Jane *(Chapter 28)*
2 Diana Rivers *(Chapter 29)*
3 Jane *(Chapter 29)*
4 St John Rivers *(Chapter 30)*
5 St John *(Chapter 33)*
6 St John *(Chapter 32)*
7 Rosamund Oliver *(Chapter 32)*
8 Jane *(Chapter 34)*

TEST YOURSELF (Chapters 36–38)

A 1 Jane *(Chapter 34)*
2 Jane *(Chapter 37)*
3 Rochester *(Chapter 37)*
4 Rochester *(Chapter 37)*
5 Bertha *(Chapter 36)*
6 Rochester *(Chapter 37)*
7 St John *(Chapter 37)*

GCSE and equivalent levels (£3.50 each)

Maya Angelou
I Know Why the Caged Bird Sings

Jane Austen
Pride and Prejudice

Harold Brighouse
Hobson's Choice

Charlotte Brontë
Jane Eyre

Emily Brontë
Wuthering Heights

Charles Dickens
David Copperfield

Charles Dickens
Great Expectations

Charles Dickens
Hard Times

George Eliot
Silas Marner

William Golding
Lord of the Flies

Willis Hall
The Long and the Short and the Tall

Thomas Hardy
Far from the Madding Crowd

Thomas Hardy
The Mayor of Casterbridge

Thomas Hardy
Tess of the d'Urbervilles

L.P. Hartley
The Go-Between

Seamus Heaney
Selected Poems

Susan Hill
I'm the King of the Castle

Barry Hines
A Kestrel for a Knave

Louise Lawrence
Children of the Dust

Harper Lee
To Kill a Mockingbird

Laurie Lee
Cider with Rosie

Arthur Miller
A View from the Bridge

Arthur Miller
The Crucible

Robert O'Brien
Z for Zachariah

George Orwell
Animal Farm

J.B. Priestley
An Inspector Calls

Willy Russell
Educating Rita

Willy Russell
Our Day Out

J.D. Salinger
The Catcher in the Rye

William Shakespeare
Henry V

William Shakespeare
Julius Caesar

William Shakespeare
Macbeth

William Shakespeare
A Midsummer Night's Dream

William Shakespeare
The Merchant of Venice

William Shakespeare
Romeo and Juliet

William Shakespeare
The Tempest

William Shakespeare
Twelfth Night

George Bernard Shaw
Pygmalion

R.C. Sherriff
Journey's End

Rukshana Smith
Salt on the snow

John Steinbeck
Of Mice and Men

R.L. Stevenson
Dr Jekyll and Mr Hyde

Robert Swindells
Daz 4 Zoe

Mildred D. Taylor
Roll of Thunder, Hear My Cry

Mark Twain
The Adventures of Huckleberry Finn

James Watson
Talking in Whispers

A Choice of Poets

Nineteenth Century Short Stories

Poetry of the First World War

Six Women Poets

Advanced level (£3.99 each)

Margaret Atwood
The Handmaid's Tale

William Blake
Songs of Innocence and of Experience

Emily Brontë
Wuthering Heights

Geoffrey Chaucer
The Wife of Bath's Prologue and Tale

Joseph Conrad
Heart of Darkness

Charles Dickens
Great Expectations

F. Scott Fitzgerald
The Great Gatsby

Thomas Hardy
Tess of the d'Urbervilles

James Joyce
Dubliners

Arthur Miller
Death of a Salesman

William Shakespeare
Antony and Cleopatra

William Shakespeare
Hamlet

William Shakespeare
King Lear

William Shakespeare
The Merchant of Venice

William Shakespeare
Romeo and Juliet

William Shakespeare
The Tempest

Mary Shelley
Frankenstein

Alice Walker
The Color Purple

Tennessee Williams
A Streetcar Named Desire

Jane Austen
Emma

Jane Austen
Pride and Prejudice

Charlotte Brontë
Jane Eyre

Seamus Heaney
Selected Poems

William Shakespeare
Much Ado About Nothing

William Shakespeare
Othello

John Webster
The Duchess of Malfi

Chinua Achebe
Things Fall Apart

Edward Albee
Who's Afraid of Virginia Woolf?

Jane Austen
Mansfield Park

Jane Austen
Northanger Abbey

Jane Austen
Persuasion

Jane Austen
Sense and Sensibility

Samuel Beckett
Waiting for Godot

Alan Bennett
Talking Heads

John Betjeman
Selected Poems

Robert Bolt
A Man for All Seasons

Robert Burns
Selected Poems

Lord Byron
Selected Poems

Geoffrey Chaucer
The Franklin's Tale

Geoffrey Chaucer
The Merchant's Tale

Geoffrey Chaucer
The Miller's Tale

Geoffrey Chaucer
The Nun's Priest's Tale

Geoffrey Chaucer
Prologue to the Canterbury Tales

Samuel Taylor Coleridge
Selected Poems

Daniel Defoe
Moll Flanders

Daniel Defoe
Robinson Crusoe

Shelagh Delaney
A Taste of Honey

Charles Dickens
Bleak House

Charles Dickens
Oliver Twist

Emily Dickinson
Selected Poems

John Donne
Selected Poems

Douglas Dunn
Selected Poems

George Eliot
Middlemarch

George Eliot
The Mill on the Floss

T.S. Eliot
The Waste Land

T.S. Eliot
Selected Poems

Henry Fielding
Joseph Andrews

E.M. Forster
Howards End

E.M. Forster
A Passage to India

John Fowles
The French Lieutenant's Woman

Brian Friel
Translations

Elizabeth Gaskell
North and South

Oliver Goldsmith
She Stoops to Conquer

Graham Greene
Brighton Rock

Thomas Hardy
Jude the Obscure

Thomas Hardy
Selected Poems

Nathaniel Hawthorne
The Scarlet Letter

Ernest Hemingway
The Old Man and the Sea

Homer
The Iliad

Homer
The Odyssey

Aldous Huxley
Brave New World

Ben Jonson
The Alchemist

Ben Jonson
Volpone

James Joyce
A Portrait of the Artist as a Young Man

John Keats
Selected Poems

Philip Larkin
Selected Poems

D.H. Lawrence
The Rainbow

D.H. Lawrence
Sons and Lovers

D.H. Lawrence
Women in Love

Christopher Marlowe
Doctor Faustus

John Milton
Paradise Lost Bks I & II

John Milton
Paradise Lost IV & IX

Sean O'Casey
Juno and the Paycock

George Orwell
Nineteen Eighty-four

John Osborne
Look Back in Anger

Wilfred Owen
Selected Poems

Harold Pinter
The Caretaker

Sylvia Plath
Selected Works

Alexander Pope
Selected Poems

Jean Rhys
Wide Sargasso Sea

William Shakespeare
As You Like It

William Shakespeare
Coriolanus

William Shakespeare
Henry IV Pt 1

William Shakespeare
Henry V

William Shakespeare
Julius Caesar

William Shakespeare
Measure for Measure

William Shakespeare
Much Ado About Nothing

William Shakespeare
A Midsummer Night's Dream

William Shakespeare
Richard II

William Shakespeare
Richard III

William Shakespeare
Sonnets

William Shakespeare
The Taming of the Shrew

William Shakespeare
The Winter's Tale

George Bernard Shaw
Arms and the Man

George Bernard Shaw
Saint Joan

Richard Brinsley Sheridan
The Rivals

Muriel Spark
The Prime of Miss Jean Brodie

John Steinbeck
The Grapes of Wrath

John Steinbeck
The Pearl

Tom Stoppard
Rosencrantz and Guildenstern are Dead

Jonathan Swift
Gulliver's Travels

John Millington Synge
The Playboy of the Western World

W.M. Thackeray
Vanity Fair

Virgil
The Aeneid

Derek Walcott
Selected Poems

Oscar Wilde
The Importance of Being Earnest

Tennessee Williams
Cat on a Hot Tin Roof

Tennessee Williams
The Glass Menagerie

Virginia Woolf
Mrs Dalloway

Virginia Woolf
To the Lighthouse

William Wordsworth
Selected Poems

W.B. Yeats
Selected Poems

York Notes – the Ultimate Literature Guides

York Notes are recognised as the best literature study guides.
If you have enjoyed using this book and have found it useful, you
can now order others directly from us – simply follow the ordering
instructions below.

HOW TO ORDER

Decide which title(s) you require and then order in one of the following
ways:

Booksellers
All titles available from good bookstores.

By post
List the title(s) you require in the space provided overleaf,
select your method of payment, complete your name and
address details and return your completed order form and
payment to:

> *Addison Wesley Longman Ltd*
> *PO BOX 88*
> *Harlow*
> *Essex CM19 5SR*

By phone
Call our Customer Information Centre on 01279 623923 to
place your order, quoting mail number: HEYN1.

By fax
Complete the order form overleaf, ensuring you fill in your
name and address details and method of payment, and fax it
to us on 01279 414130.

By e-mail
E-mail your order to us on awlhe.orders@awl.co.uk listing
title(s) and quantity required and providing full name and
address details as requested overleaf. Please quote mail
number: HEYN1. Please do not send credit card details by
e-mail.

York Notes Order Form

Titles required:

Quantity	Title/ISBN	Price

Sub total _____

Please add £2.50 postage & packing _____

(*P & P is free for orders over £50*) _____

Total _____

Mail no: HEYN1

Your Name _____

Your Address _____

Postcode _____ Telephone _____

Method of payment

☐ I enclose a cheque or a P/O for £_____ made payable to Addison Wesley Longman Ltd

☐ Please charge my Visa/Access/AMEX/Diners Club card

Number _____ Expiry Date _____

Signature _____ Date _____

(please ensure that the address given above is the same as for your credit card)

Prices and other details are correct at time of going to press but may change without notice. All orders are subject to status.

☐ *Please tick this box if you would like a complete listing of Longman Study Guides (suitable for GCSE and A-level students)*

York Press

Longman

Addison Wesley Longman